ITEM 018 338 944

D0245080

UXBRIDGE College Learning Centre
Coldharbour Lane, Hayes, Middlesex UB3 3BB
Telephone: 01895 853740

Please return this item to the Learning Centre
on or before the last date stamped below:

UXBRIDGE · COLLEGE

0 1 JUL 2011
0 7 JAN 2014
0 4 FEB 2014

942.19

LEARNING RESOURCES AT UXBRIDGE COLLEGE

UXBRIDGE COLLEGE LIBRARY

Memories
of
Uxbridge

Part of the
Memories
series

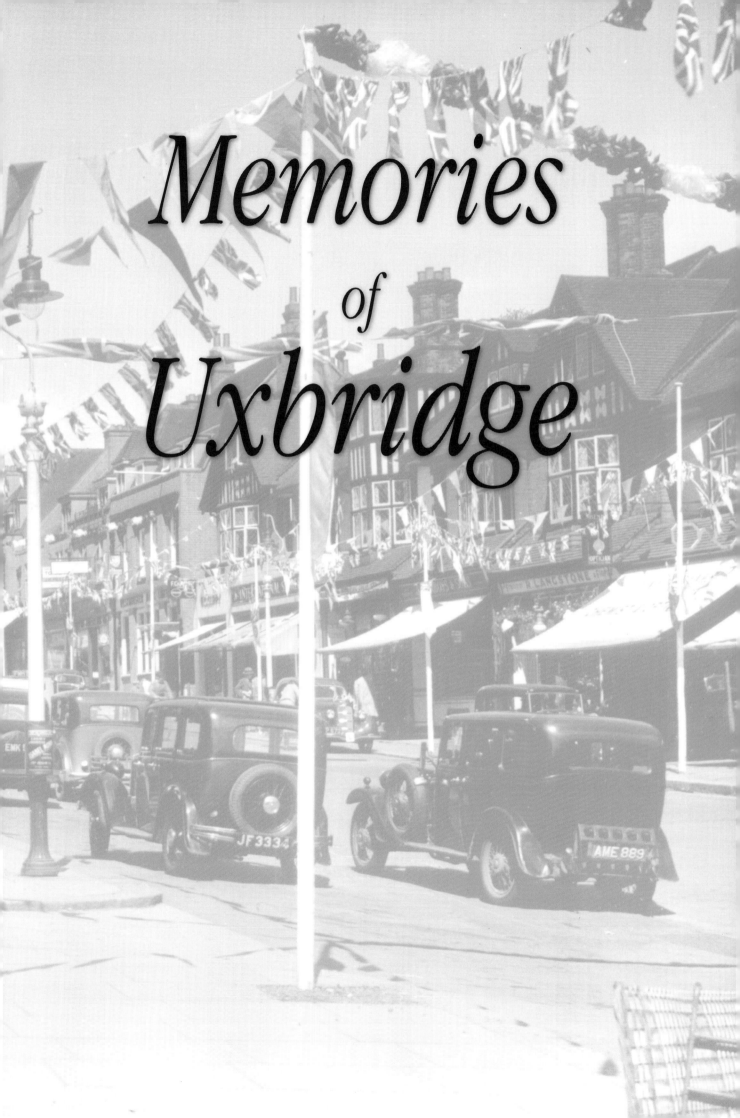

Memories
of
Uxbridge

*The Publishers would like to thank the following companies for supporting
the production of this book*

Main Sponsor

Brunel University

Bickerton's Aerodromes Limited

JR Parsons Limited

Pavilions Shopping Centre

Pictorialist Euro Foto Centre

Toolmasters Technologies Limited

The WOODBRIDGE Partnership

First published in Great Britain by True North Books Limited
Units 3 - 5 Heathfield Industrial Park
Elland West Yorkshire
HX5 9AE
Tel. 01422 377977
© Copyright: True North Books Limited 1999

All rights reserved. No part of this publication may be reproduced, stored in a retrieval system, or transmitted in any
form, or by any means, electronic, mechanical, photocopy, recording or otherwise without the prior permission in
writing of the Copyright holders, nor be otherwise circulated in any form or binding or cover other than in which it is
published and without a similar condition being imposed on the subsequent publisher.

ISBN 1 900463 64 4

*Text, design and origination by True North Books Limited
Printed and bound by The Amadeus Press Limited*

Memories are made of this

Memories. We all have them; some good, some bad, but our memories of the town we grew up in are usually tucked away in a very special place in our minds. The best are usually connected with our childhood and youth, when we longed to be grown up and paid no attention to adults who told us to enjoy being young, as these were the best years of our lives. We look back now and realise that they were right.

So many memories - perhaps of the war and rationing, perhaps of parades, celebrations and royal visits. And so many changes; one-way traffic systems and pedestrianisation. New trends in shopping that led to the very first self-serve stores being opened.

Through the bad times and the good, however, Uxbridge not only survived but prospered. We have only to look at the town as it is today, to see what progress has been realised and what achievements have been made over the last 50 years. Uxbridge has a history to be proud of - but more importantly, a great future to look forward to, into the new millennium and beyond.

Contents

Around the town centre

This marvellous old photograph takes us on a trip back through time to the early 1930s and the echoes of Uxbridge's rural past. Vernon Brown & Co were one of those stores where you could not only buy most things you needed to take care of your pets, but your gardening supplies also. The shop was an agent for Spratts, and had an awesome list of poultry foods, cage bird supplies, pet foods, corn, seeds and manure for sale.

At the time, Uxbridge had a flourishing cut flower industry that dated back to the years before World War I. The largest supplier was Lowe and Shawyers, who eventually became the largest employer in the district, with more than 300 on their staff. Brunel University today occupies the site.

But at Vernon Brown's thriving stores, the small gardener was not forgotten, and your 'tulips from Amsterdam', golden yellow, crimson and any other colour you liked, could be purchased along with every other kind of bulb to brighten up your springtime. At the time of the photograph, the store already occupied numbers 145 and 146, while the adjoining 147 stood vacant. By 1933 Vernon Brown & Co had expanded into these premises also.

Bottom: Changes were afoot in the town when this photograph was taken, possibly in the early 1930s.... So what's new? The window of F F Poole, family butcher, was boarded up, as were the adjoining two properties, though it is not clear from the photograph exactly what was going on. Readers who grew up in Uxbridge will need few reminders of Welch and Gibbs, though its position on the 'wrong' side of the High Street may confuse them for a few minutes until they realise that the well-known outfitter eventually moved to its more familiar position.

How many readers remember their school days, when their mothers cajoled them into a visit to Welch and Gibbs, where they were kitted out in the uniforms of Bishopshalt Grammar school and other upper schools in the area? By that time, the long school holidays were almost at an end, and that sinking 'back to school' feeling was tinged with the excitement of starting afresh in a different year, or even a different school. Those were the days!

Right: A well-dressed lady stops to allow this Commer delivery van to pass on its way down Windsor street. The year is 1928, and though these distinctive early motor vehicles evoke those wistful 'good old days' feelings, the solid rubber tyres which many still had, and the solid beam axle, together with the cobbled roads, would have made for a teeth-chattering ride! Vans

of as little as one and a half tons capacity were fitted with solid tyres; on roads which still had many horse-shoe nails lying around, they were practical if not comfortable. The top speed of vehicles like this one would have been around 20 miles per hour.

Pictured here at 40 Windsor Street is J Hutton's 'noted fish supper bar'. In the 1920s a nutritious fish and chip supper would set you back a couple of coppers, a bargain even in those days, though the hard-up were at times driven to ask for 'a ha'pennorth of each'.... The lady crossing the road does not, however, appear to be among the poor, and in spite of the bright sunshine she is wearing her winter coat, with fur collar and cuffs.

Electronic keyboards complete with headphones and computer discs were far in the future on the day a photographer recorded the windows of Willis & Sons for posterity. Willis & Sons was a high-class musical instrument store well known to all Uxbridge's music lovers, who might have bought a piano there together with the sheet music of the latest popular song. Willis & Son also offered a piano tuning and repair service to back up their sales. The photograph was taken in 1929, a time when

The BBC made its first radio broadcast on 15th November 1922

radio was in its infancy (the BBC made its first broadcast on 15th November 1922), and across the country families still gathered around the piano in the evenings for a singsong. Until that year, the piano played a vital part in many cinemas - but 1929 saw the advent of the 'talkies', and it was the end of the road for the old cinema pianists. Theatre tickets could also be obtained at Willis & Sons for the Chiswick Empire, and one of the many informative posters in the window tells passers by that 'All at Sea' was playing in the near future.

Events of the 1930s

HOT OFF THE PRESS
The years of the 1930s saw Adolf Hitler's sickening anti-Jewish campaign echoed in the streets of Britain. On 19th October 1936 Oswald Mosley's 7,000-strong British Union of Fascists clashed head on with thousands of Jews and Communists in London, resulting in 80 people being injured in the ensuing battle. Mosley and his 'blackshirts' later rampaged through the streets beating up Jews and smashing the windows of their businesses.

GETTING AROUND
At the beginning of the decade many believed that the airship was the transport of the future. The R101 airship, however, loaded with thousands of cubic metres of hydrogen, crashed in France on its maiden flight in 1930. Forty-eight passengers and crew lost their lives. In 1937 the Hindenburg burst into flames - the entire disaster caught on camera and described by a distraught reporter. The days of the airship were numbered.

SPORTING CHANCE
In 1939 British racing driver Sir Malcolm Campbell hit the headlines when he captured the world's water-speed record for the third time in 'Bluebird' - all his cars were given the same name. A racing driver who set world speed records both on land and on water, Sir Malcolm established world land-speed records no fewer than nine times. His son Donald went on to set further records, tragically dying in 1967 when his speedboat - also named 'Bluebird' - crashed.

How many readers remember Uxbridge before towering glass and concrete replaced so many of its old buildings? This long-ago view of Windsor Street, captured from St Margaret's tower, will bring back many memories to those who appreciate a trip down Memory Lane, perhaps to view the Old Bill when it was still the town's police station. (Who can recall the air raid siren that was mounted on the roof

during the second world war?) St Margaret's was built in 1248, and was extended around 1400. In a town which lost so much of its original character in the move towards the modern age, the old church, while providing us with a solid and comforting link to the past, at the same time has kept in touch with real life.

The Nave project, launched by Prime Minister Margaret Thatcher in 1989, demonstrates exactly how the church can cater for the needs of people living at the beginning of a new millennium. Music events, celebrity visits, exhibitions - and a tasteful coffee bar - are all part of the ministry of St Margaret's.

As we look across the rooftops towards the Gas Works in Cowley Road, we can see that Windsor street is busy with people going about their everyday lives: taking a trip to the shops, walking to work, wheeling out the babies in their prams. The Queen's Head is off-picture to the right and is still a pleasant watering hole today. The Pavilions shopping centre, which was to replace many of these streets, was undreamed of at the time of this nostalgic photograph. The view, probably dating from the 1930s or even the 20s, includes no private cars, and the only motor vehicles in sight are delivery wagons. Those were the days when horse-drawn carts were only beginning to be overtaken by motorised transport, and the only kind of traffic pollution could be collected and used on your floribunda! Those wonderful old horse-drawn vehicles could be seen around our streets, carrying anything from bags of coal to milk, well into the 1940s and even, in some places, the 1950s. The photograph - unfortunately undated - was taken from the tower of St Margaret's church, which houses the famous peal of eight bells.

Randalls store has been a well known landmark in Uxbridge for many years

Few people were out and about when this scene was caught on camera. We have no date for the photograph, but trams were still passing along the High Street at the time. It was perhaps taken to record the newly rebuilt Randalls store - a well known landmark in the town for many years, and where you can still buy anything from a dinner service to a bedroom carpet. Note the solitary bicycle which has been left standing at the kerb outside what became Bird and Lovibond's premises;

those were the gentler days when you could leave your bike behind while you popped off to do a little shopping, then expect to find the bike still there when you returned.

At the time Vine Street was very different from the place we know today. As well as the railway station, many shops, pubs and businesses were based in the busy little street, including, in the 1920s, a factory run by a certain Miss W Thomas, where evening wear and blouses were made for the big London stores. The factory employed between 25 and 30 girls.

Blink, and you miss it...the sad passing of yet another of Uxbridge's old and well-loved watering-holes! Young's newsagents has hardly changed at all in the second photograph *(inset)* and you somehow get the feeling that even the newspaper headlines should be the same. A pile of rubble is all that is left of the Great Western,

and it seems almost hard-hearted of Youngs to use their now exposed gable end for advertising purposes! The Great Western, sacrificed in the name of progress, was at one time one of the town's important inns, with a long history that stretched back to the early 16th century. Benskins was a Watford brewery which itself

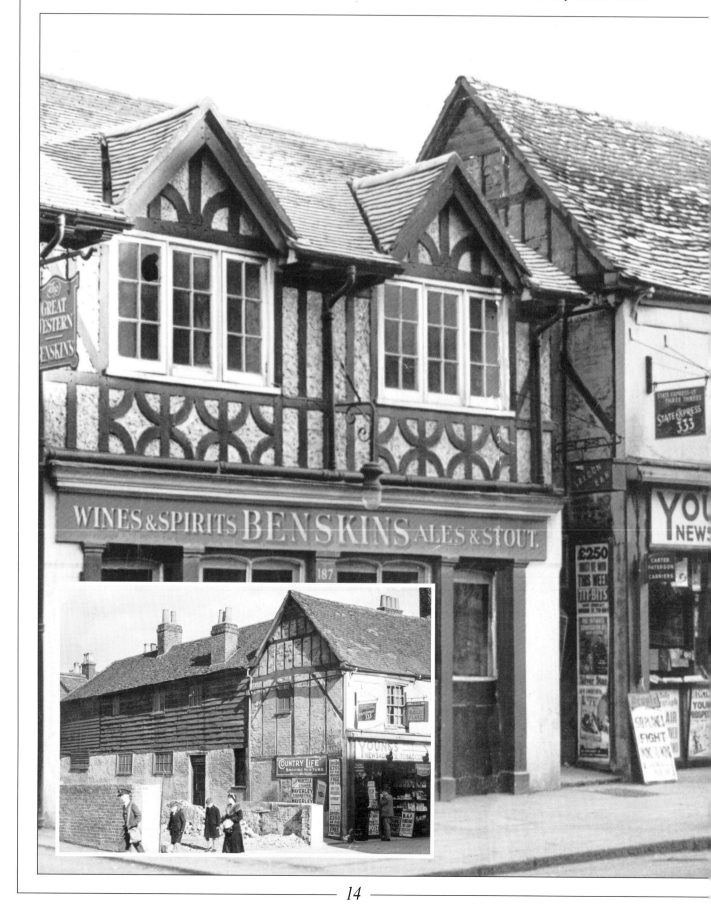

dates back more than 100 years. Joseph Benskin was just 13 years old when he got a job in the hotel trade, and hard work and a keen mind enabled him to carve out a successful career in the business. In 1867 he moved to Watford, where he founded the brewery that was to make his name famous. In 1957 the company merged with Ind Coope, and today they are part of Allied Breweries.

Events of the 1930s

SCIENCE AND DISCOVERY
By observing the heavens, astronomers had long believed that there in the constellation of Gemini lay a new planet, so far undiscovered. They began to search for the elusive planet, and a special astronomical camera was built for the purpose. The planet Pluto was discovered by amateur astronomer Clyde Tombaugh in 1930, less than a year later.

WHAT'S ON?
In this heyday of the cinema, horrified audiences were left gasping at the sight of Fay Wray in the clutches of the giant ape in the film 'King Kong', released in 1933. Very different but just as gripping was the gutsy 1939 American Civil War romance 'Gone with the Wind'. Gable's parting words, 'Frankly, my dear, I don't give a damn' went down in history. 1936 - Britain set up the world's first television service - black and white, of course. The Queen's coronation in 1953, the first such ceremony to be televised, did much to popularise television.

ROYAL WATCH
The talking point of the early 1930s was the affair of the Prince of Wales, who later became King Edward VIII, and American divorcee Wallis Simpson. Faced with a choice, Edward gave up his throne for 'the woman I love' and spent the remainder of his life in exile. Many supported him, though they might not have been as keen to do so if they had been aware of his Nazi sympathies, kept strictly under wraps at the time.

How many readers remember sampling their first pint in the Kings Arms in the High Street? The Kings Arms was an old coaching inn (possibly called The Rose at one time), with a long history that went way back to the 15th century. The pub eventually became a Grade II listed building, but the sighs of relief gave way to groans of 'What's the point?' when the developers' red pen changed for ever the face of yet another piece of Uxbridge's history. The Kings Arms closed in 1960 and its frontage was later drastically altered. Adjoining the pub was the International Stores, provision merchants, whose trade would undoubtedly have suffered when Uxbridge's first self service stores opened. This was the 1950s, and sweeping changes in shopping were about to hit not only Uxbridge but towns and cities across the UK. Do you remember how strange it felt, picking up a wire basket and helping yourself from the goods on display on the shelves - it was almost like stealing! It was, however, only the thin end of the wedge, and the trend towards out of town shopping sounded the death knell for many smaller chains and little corner shops.

Above: In the 20th century the fine building we know today as the premises of Bird & Lovibond, solicitors, was the private home of *the* Mr W Randall, of department store fame. The character of Vine Street was quite different during those the early years, and the railway station provided the nearby shops and services with a regular supply of potential customers. Road widening was in progress when this photograph was taken in March 1939, as was some renovation work on the building, and a painter adds the necessary finishing touches to one of the windows.

In the background of the photograph, tucked away on the High Street the name 'Bata' outlined against a white background immediately attracts the eye - surely a good marketing ploy? There was a time when high streets around the country were sprinkled with an assortment of different shoe shops: Freeman, Hardy and Willis, Saxone, Dolcis, Timpson, Stead and Simpson, Barratts, Bata - there they all were. Is it imagination, or are there fewer shoe shops about today?

The old market hall is one of the few features of Uxbridge High Street which is still recognisable, though today's traders operate from a number of separate shops within the facility. What an amazing place this must have been when it was built in the 18th century, when traders set up their stalls and sold their many and varied wares from beneath the building's stately pillars. Certainly noisy - and perhaps smelly too! This market building replaced a smaller 16th century market, though Uxbridge was granted the right to hold a market as early

as the late 1100s. The picturesque market building might have had a long history, but the average working day was often a less than pleasant experience for the traders whose livelihood depended on their standing around for hour after hour in the chill winds of winter.

During the 1970s an experiment was made to enclose the ground floor, but the result was unattractive and did nothing to enhance the building, and it was subsequently removed. Later developments led to today's sensitive and more pleasant approach to the problem.

Above: How many readers remember holding hands with their latest date on the back row of the Savoy? The thousand-seat picture palace opened on 3rd October 1921 with the silent film 'Romance', which starred Doris Keane. No honky-tonk piano accompanied the programme - an orchestra provided the background music for the film. Television took off in a big way during the 1950s and sadly spelled the beginning of the end for the local cinemas that were dotted around the town. The Savoy, pictured here during its final week, was the first to go, and its farewell programme included 'Doctor in the House' and 'Man of the Moment'. The comedy 'Doctor in the House', starring Dirk Bogarde and Kenneth More, attracted rave reviews when it was produced in 1954, and many sequels naturally followed the successful film. Norman Wisdom - still going strong today - was the star of the slapstick comedy 'Man of the Moment'. Ladbrokes took over the Savoy, and after its closure on 18th June 1960 the old cinema went eyes down to bingo. The building was demolished in 1982 and today the Royal Bank of Scotland stands in the same position.

This thought-provoking view of Mahjacks Corner was captured as demolition of many of the surrounding old buildings was still in progress. Local DIY enthusiasts still think wistfully of Mahjacks - virtually the only place where you could wander round and browse among their marvellous range of goodies, and come away with half a dozen galvanised nails, an odd cup hook and a couple of wood screws - a facility sadly missed today, when nails, screws and the like come in little plastic packs, with far more in them than you need for the job! As the new millennium approached, this land still lay vacant, with rumours of further office blocks in the wind.

On a different theme, it is interesting to note that the only pedestrian in the scene is ignoring the zebra crossing, though she appears to be in no immediate danger from passing traffic. The first zebra crossings were introduced in Uxbridge High Street in 1952, though pedestrian crossings, the invention of the Minister of Transport, Leslie Hore Belisha, had been part and parcel of life in Britain since 1934.

CABINET FITTINGS
FORMICA

IRONMONGERY
TOOLS

HARDBOARD
TIMBER

MAHJACKS
CORNER

UXBRIDGE 3262

Windsor Street is one of the few places in Uxbridge that still retains much of its old charm and character - even the Old Bill public house has been tastefully created to retain the features of the old police station. During the 1960s Webb's leather and grindery merchants was a convenient spot to drop off your shoes for repair, or to buy a new purse or leather wallet. A very different kind of business was to eventually replace the old shoe repair shop.... Of especial interest in this 1968 shot is the little Mini, still cherished today by the many affectionate owners who managed to hang on to theirs. The Mini

was introduced to British drivers in 1959 by Alexander Issigonis in response to Germany's popular VW Beetle. The Mini's transverse engine made it possible to seat four passengers in comfort in spite of the car only being an incredible ten feet in length. The little vehicle was practical, affordable and fuel-efficient - all features that established it as a firm favourite, especially with the student population and other hard-up younger drivers. Issigonis was knighted in 1969 for his contribution to British design, and by the time he died in 1988 more than five million Minis had been sold.

Wartime

In 1939 Britain's Prime Minister Neville Chamberlain had made his announcement to the waiting people of Britain that '...this country is at war with Germany.' Uxbridge, along with the rest of the country rolled up its sleeves and prepared for the inevitable. This war would be different from other wars. This time planes had the ability to fly further and carry a heavier load, and air raids were fully expected. Air raid shelters were obviously going to be needed, and shelters were built on open places across the town.

By the time war was declared an army of volunteers of both sexes had already been recruited to form an Air Raid Protection service. At first ARP personnel were unpaid volunteers but when war broke out in September 1939 they became paid staff. It was their job to patrol specified areas, making sure that no chinks of light broke the blackout restrictions, checking the safety of local residents, being alert for gas attacks, air raids and unexploded bombs. The exceptional work done by Air Raid Wardens in dealing with incendiaries, giving first aid to the injured, helping to rescue victims from their bombed-out properties, clearing away rubble, and a thousand and one other tasks became legendary; during the second world war nearly as many private citizens were killed as troops - and many of them were the gallant ARP wardens.

At the beginning of the war Sir Anthony Eden, Secretary of State for War, appealed in a radio broadcast for men between 17 and 65 to make up a new force, the Local Defence Volunteers, to guard vulnerable points from possible Nazi attack. Within a very short time the first men were putting their names down. At first the new force had to improvise; there were no weapons to spare and men had to rely on sticks, shotguns handed in by local people, and on sheer determination . Weapons and uniforms did not become available for several months.

In July the Local Defence Volunteers was renamed the Home Guard, and by the following year were a force to be reckoned with. Television programmes such as 'Dad's Army' have unfortunately associated the Home Guard with comedy, but in fact they performed much important work. The Guard posted sentries to watch for possible aircraft or parachute landings at likely spots such as disused aerodromes, golf courses on the outskirts of towns, local parks and racecourses. They manned anti-aircraft rocket guns, liaised with other units and with regular troops, set up communications and organised balloon barrages.

Other preparations were hastily made around the town. Place names and other identifying marks were obliterated to confuse the enemy about exactly where they were. Notices went up everywhere giving good advice to citizens on a number of issues. 'Keep Mum - she's not so dumb' warned people to take care what kind of information they passed on, as the person they were speaking to could be an enemy.

Older readers will remember how difficult it was to find certain items in the shops during the war; combs, soap, cosmetics, hairgrips, elastic, buttons, zips - all were virtually impossible to buy as factories that once produced these items had been turned over to war work. Stockings were in short supply, and resourceful women resorted to colouring their legs with gravy browning or with a mixture of sand and water. Beetroot juice was found to be a good substitute for lipstick.

Clothes rationing was introduced in 1941, and everyone had 66 coupons per year. Eleven coupons would buy a dress, and sixteen were needed for a coat. The number of coupons was later reduced to 40 per person. People were required to save material where they could - ladies' hemlines went up considerably, and skirts were not allowed to have lots of pleats. Some found clever ways around the regulations by using materials that were not rationed. Blackout material could be embroidered and made into blouses or skirts, and dyed sugar sacks were turned into curtains.

Above: War had been declared, and every citizen of Britain, young and old, male and female, was called upon to put his or her back into the war effort. Those who did not go into military service of one kind or another worked in factories, dug for victory, gave up their aluminium baths and saucepans, joined organisations and aided in any way they could. These boys from were not going to be left out; they might be too young to fight but while there were sandbags to be filled they were going to do their bit to protect their school building. Thousands of sandbags were used during World War II to protect the country and its beautiful civic buildings.

Left: A proud father poses for the camera with his latest arrival. The baby had not arrived from Mars, in fact the 'arrival' was not a baby at all, but an anti-gas attack suit which was compulsory for babies in the United Kingdom during the second world war. An air pump at the side of the suit enabled anxious parents to replenish the supply of air to the precious package inside. It is said that most babies were less than enthusiastic abut the prospect of being encased in the suit - and who could blame them? The picture was taken in 1939. In the event there was never any gas attack on British soil during the course of the second world war.

Events of the 1930s

MELODY MAKERS

Throughout the 1930s a young American trombonist called Glenn Miller was making his mark in the world of music. By 1939 the Glenn Miller sound was a clear leader in the field; his clean-cut, meticulously executed arrangements of numbers such as 'A String of Pearls' and 'Moonlight Serenade' brought him fame across the world as a big-band leader. During a flight to England from Paris in 1944 Miller's plane disappeared; no wreckage was ever found.

THE WORLD AT LARGE

In India, Gandhi's peaceful protests against British rule were gathering momentum. The Salt Laws were a great bone of contention: forced to buy salt from the British government, thousands of protestors marched to the salt works, intending to take it over in the name of the Indian people. Policemen and guards attacked the marchers, but not one of them fought back. Gandhi, who earned for himself the name 'Mahatma' - Great Soul - was assassinated in 1948.

INVENTION AND TECHNOLOGY

With no driving tests or speed restrictions, 120,000 people were killed on the roads in Britain between the two world wars. In 1934 Percy Shaw, invented a safety device destined to become familiar the world over: reflecting roadstuds. In dark or foggy conditions the studs that reflected light from the car's headlights kept traffic on the 'straight and narrow' and must over the years have saved many lives.

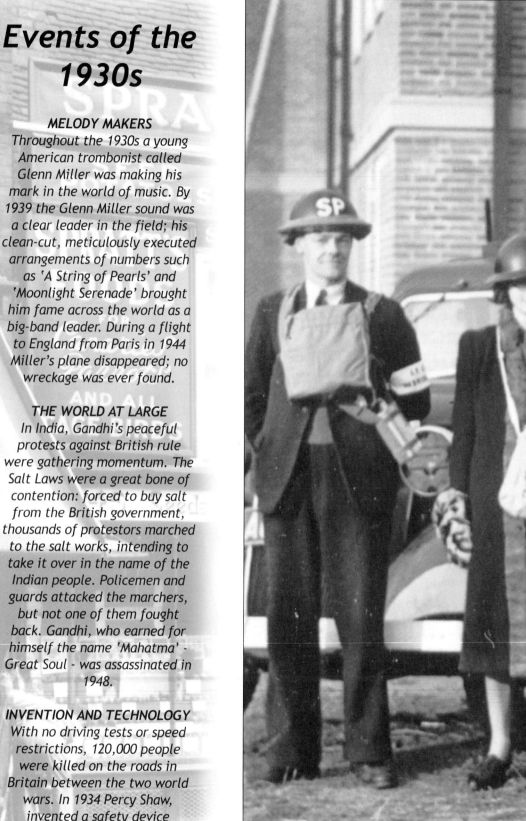

St John Ambulance Society and Red Cross ambulance units are pictured here outside the County offices. The date was 20th January 1940, and in the 'calm before the storm' the second world war was getting into gear. This cheerful group of workers and their colleagues would be at the sharp end of the rescue work when the reality of war hit Uxbridge. In case of enemy attack, it was thought to be important for the ordinary person in

the street to have at least a basic knowledge of first-aid, and it was people like the members of these ambulance units who were needed to pass on their skills. Knowing how to stop bleeding, treat gas contamination, bandage a limb, treat burns and scalds, dress wounds and treat shock, was a dreadful necessity during wartime.

Before war was declared a little book called 'The Protection of your Home against Air Raids' was sent to every home in Britain to alert the general public to the dangers they might have to face. A list of simple first aid supplies was given, and every home was advised to have lint, cotton wool, bandages and iodine on hand.

Both pictures: The 'paper sucking' exercise is in progress, and a photographer catches the test that proves the efficiency of the gas masks, being fitted here on 27th September 1938 by Miss Dorothy Royle, headmistress of Whitehall Infants School *(left)*. Most of these little girls appear to be taking the exercise in their stride, though the little girl on the right doesn't look too sure.... Elsewhere (was this Bishop-shalt School?), a group of boys queue across the front of the classroom to be fitted with theirs by headmaster Mr Pentrey *(Below)*.

War had not yet been declared when the local school children were fitted with their masks - an enormous task, carried out by a couple of air raid wardens and the school staff.

Gas attack was the big fear at the start of World War II, and before the war began millions of gas masks had already been manufactured. Germany had used gas during World War I and it was fully expected that they would do so again.

Young children were often frightened by the fearsome look of the gas masks, and the tots were given blue and red 'Mickey Mouse' masks complete with ears. Babies under two were provided with special gas helmets.

Notices were posted everywhere to remind people to carry their masks with them, though it was not compulsory under the law. Some cinemas and theatres, however, refused to admit people who did not have their masks with them. The notice 'Hitler will send no warning - so always carry your gas mask' emphasised the danger. At first people carried them wherever they went. They attended regular refresher courses, many held by firms during working hours, to make sure they could put on their masks speedily, and they attended sessions held to test the efficiency of their masks. Within a few months, however, the fear of gas was receding and the masks were increasingly being left hanging on a peg behind the front door at home.

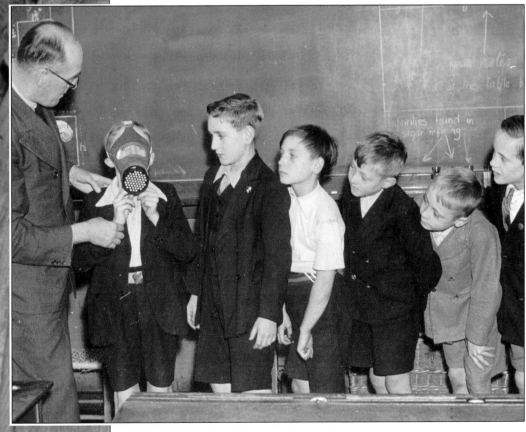

Long before war was declared in September 1939 it was realised that this new conflict would be largely fought in the skies. In response, the Air Raid Precautions service was set up, and in Uxbridge Dragonfield, near the Uxbridge UDC offices, became the local headquarters. A large number of people would eventually be needed to act as air raid officials, and the first of the new ARP officers was Captain Emerson. A total of 44 wardens posts were set up around the town and an army of volunteers of both sexes was recruited to the service, probably the largest percentage of them coming from the upper and middle classes. Some exceptional work was done by Air Raid Wardens during the war when they dealt with incendi-

aries, gave first aid to the injured, helped to rescue victims from their bombed-out properties, cleared away rubble, and performed a thousand and one other tasks.

The photograph, taken during an ARP exercise in January 1941, captures a number of officials, tin hats at the ready. Among them were John Poole, Clerk to Uxbridge UDC, W Pomeroy, Chairman of the UDC, Mr Jackson of the ARP and Mr Tramell, Deputy Clerk.

Events of the 1940s

WHAT'S ON?

In wartime Britain few families were without a wireless set. It was the most popular form of entertainment, and programmes such as ITMA, Music While You Work and Workers' Playtime provided the people with an escape from the harsh realities of bombing raids and ration books. In 1946 the BBC introduced the Light Programme, the Home Service and the Third Programme, which gave audiences a wider choice of listening.

GETTING AROUND

October 1948 saw the production of Britain's first new car designs since before the war. The Morris Minor was destined for fame as one of the most popular family cars, while the four-wheel-drive Land Rover answered the need for a British-made off-road vehicle. The country was deeply in the red, however, because of overseas debts incurred during the war. The post-war export drive that followed meant that British drivers had a long wait for their own new car.

SPORTING CHANCE

American World Heavyweight Boxing Champion Joe Louis, who first took the title back in 1937, ruled the world of boxing during the 1930s and 40s, making a name for himself as unbeatable. Time after time he successfully defended his title against all comers, finally retiring in 1948 after fighting an amazing 25 title bouts throughout his boxing career. Louis died in 1981 at the age of 67.

This heartbreaking pile of rubble was all that remained of homes in Rockingham Parade after an enemy raid on 28th September 1940. Six people died here, including ten year old Billy Laws and his parents, and it was thanks to the desperate efforts of courageous teams of rescuers who battled in unbelievable conditions all night, that the death toll was no higher. The George Medal was later awarded to Jack Livesey and Norman Petts, members of the 2nd Uxbridge Scout Troop, for their rescue, 'regardless of their own safety', of an elderly man who was trapped in the debris. The autumn and winter of 1940/41 saw a wave of heavy bombing in the area, and a trip to the air raid shelter became a nightly routine. Daylight raids were common throughout the winter, and workers were left wondering whether their homes would be still there at the end of the day. Those were the days when Spitfires and Hurricanes were scrambled to intercept the raiders, and dogfights took place high in the skies above Northolt.

a year, were delivered to homes around the town. Other preparations were hastily made. Gas masks were delivered, sand bags filled, blackout curtains and shutters made, and local factories imaginatively camouflaged. Place names and other identifying marks were obscured to confuse the enemy about exactly where they were....Britain was at war once again.

Top: Children are attracted to holes in the ground as they are to any other drama, large or small, and when a V-2 missile landed in Hillingdon during the second world war they were out in force to view the bomb craters! Labelled 'Hitler's second secret weapon', the first of more than 1,000 V-2s fell on London on 8th September 1944. The chilling sound of the V-1 had struck fear into all who heard the dreaded 'doodlebugs', fearing to hear the drone of the engines cease while they were overhead...you never knew where they might plummet to earth, or whose roof they might fall on. The V-2, however, was a whole new 'ball game'; the advanced supersonic weapon, literally a bolt from the blue, was at the cutting edge of technology, destroying homes and factories and delivering death before anyone even heard its approach. The much feared V-2 missile ushered in a new age of military force.

Above: It was Sunday, 3rd September 1939, and at 11.15am Prime Minister Neville Chamberlain had made his announcement to the waiting people of Britain that '...this country is at war with Germany'. Uxbridge along with the rest of the country rolled up its sleeves and prepared for the inevitable. This war would be different from other wars; this time planes had the ability to fly further and carry a heavier load, and air raids were fully expected.

Shelters were obviously going to be needed, and the photograph shows air raid trenches being dug on Uxbridge Common. Cricketfield Road and Laundry Yard saw the first of many surface shelters built, and Anderson shelters, free to those whose income was less than £250

Hayes End was on the receiving end of a V-2 missile in September 1944, and when the dust had settled there were few slates left on the rooftops of this row of maisonettes. A solitary observer ruefully surveys the ruins, perhaps wondering how anything so seriously damaged could ever be repaired.

The V-2 was indeed a weapon to fear, though the Germans had some anxiety about the accuracy of their new missile. V-2 launches began in September 1944 and before Germany surrendered on 7th May

1945 an incredible 4,000 of the missiles had been fired against the Allies. February and March 1945 saw around 60 V-2s fall every week, killing an estimated five people per launch, making it more deadly than the V-1. There was no defence against this super-weapon, which had a warhead that weighed more than 1,600 pounds; travelling faster than sound its arrival was unexpected and lethal. The only way to combat the V-2 was to detect the launch sites and mount bombing raids against them.

Events of the 1940s

HOT OFF THE PRESS
At the end of World War II in 1945 the Allies had their first sight of the unspeakable horrors of the Nazi extermination camps they had only heard of until then. In January, 4,000 emaciated prisoners more dead than alive were liberated by the Russians from Auschwitz in Poland, where three million people, most of them Jews,were murdered. The following year 23 prominent Nazis faced justice at Nuremberg; 12 of them were sentenced to death for crimes against humanity.

THE WORLD AT LARGE
The desert area of Alamogordo in New Mexico was the scene of the first atomic bomb detonation on July 16, 1945. With an explosive power equal to more than 15,000 tons of TNT, the flash could be seen 180 miles away. President Truman judged that the bomb could secure victory over Japan with far less loss of US lives than a conventional invasion, and on 6th August the first of the new weapons was dropped on Hiroshima. Around 80,000 people died.

ROYAL WATCH
By the end of World War II, the 19-year-old Princess Elizabeth and her distant cousin Lieutenant Philip Mountbatten RN were already in love. The King and Queen approved of Elizabeth's choice of husband, though they realised that she was rather young and had not mixed with many other young men. The engagement announcement was postponed until the Princess had spent four months on tour in Africa. The couple's wedding on 20th November 1947 was a glittering occasion - the first royal pageantry since before the war.

There is nothing so good for morale during any conflict as the sight of a captured enemy plane. This satisfyingly battered BF 109 Messerschmidt plane was exhibited in Uxbridge in September 1940 in aid of the Spitfire Fund - a display that attracted crowds of local people who came to see close up exactly what British pilots were faced with. More than £3,520 was raised in the appeal.
During the war the public were asked at regular intervals to

contribute to one worthy cause or another, and this type of war effort prompted much rivalry between local firms; the larger ones might raise £20,000 for a Wellington Bomber (to be repaid after the war), while smaller companies might manage to get a couple of thousand pounds together to pay for an aeroplane wing. Collections in public houses were more modest, aspiring to £30 for a sub-machine gun or £138 for a 2,000lb bomb. A donation from an individual with a few coppers to spare might be sixpence for a rivet or perhaps four shillings for a hand grenade.

Many towns and cities actually 'bought' Spitfires for £5,000; a list of contributors to the war effort was read out over the wireless every day after the evening news.

Carrying on a good name and a great tradition

During the latter half of the 20th century, the name of Brunel University has become every bit as well-known and respected in engineering circles and beyond as was the name of Isambard Kingdom Brunel, a hundred years earlier. The reputation of each is well-deserved, being a reflection of the outstanding technical competence, the creativity and the commitment which have resulted in important advances in science and knowledge as well as in a significant improvement in the quality of life for countless people.

And now, as we enter a new millennium, Brunel University's influence extends far beyond the fields of engineering, science, technology, social sciences, education and management which were its traditional strengths. A merger with the West London Institute of Higher Education in 1995 brought performing arts, humanities, geography and earth sciences, health, social work, sport sciences and business within the University's remit, so that today students in virtually any discipline can benefit from the standards of excellence, geared closely to the needs of employers and the community at large, for which Brunel University is renowned.

This merger is the most recent in a long succession of developments which has brought the institution from modest beginnings to its current status as a major force on the UK higher education scene, and a focal point for the local community. Brunel is a major business with an annual turnover of nearly £80m, and is one of the area's largest employers, providing employment for over 2,300 people; while local individuals and organisations benefit from Brunel's excellent sporting, teaching and conference facilities in an extraordinary number of ways. The conference trade, a significant source of

income for the University, brings in hundreds of visitors who spend money in the local shops and restaurants. The main conference season runs from June to September, and fills Uxbridge with groups as diverse as robotic scientists, Home Office bureaucrats, fire-fighters, and teenage Italians improving their English.

Brunel's catering and conference services are not only popular for conferences, seminars and meetings for anywhere between four and four hundred delegates, but are ideal for wedding receptions, special birthday parties and garden parties. On the academic side, Brunel's wide spectrum of vocational courses have helped countless individuals to progress in their chosen careers, while many brand new businesses in the area enjoy the advantages of occupying office, laboratory and workshop accommodation at the Science Park. The community's leisure needs are met too; Brunel's impressive sports and training facilities, which are open to the public, include a climbing wall which is rated as one of the best in the country, and a new, air-conditioned, state-of-the-art fitness suite with more than 60 pieces of Technogym equipment including resistance machines, free weights, cardiovascular equipment and the Cardio Theatre entertainment system, all supervised by a team of fully-qualified instructors. The less energetic, however, may prefer to spend their lunchtimes and evenings relaxing at a concert, or they may choose to enrol on one of the weekly courses available at the Arts Centre, where ceramics, photography, life drawing and Ikebana are among the popular options. A stimulating series of

Above: *From left to right: John Scott Russell, Henry Wakefield, Isambard Kingdom Brunel and Lord Derby awaiting the launch of the Great Eastern Steamship.*

weekend workshops and summer schools also takes place at the Arts Centre, and each year a series of interesting exhibitions is staged at the new Beldam Gallery.

People of Uxbridge who benefit in so many ways from having Brunel University on their doorstep may be interested to read of the chain of events which led first to the creation of an institution named Brunel, and then to its estab-lishment in Uxbridge. In fact the first major step was taken in 1928, when Middlesex County Council transferred its Junior Technical School, founded in Chiswick in 1910, to Acton. Here it grew rapidly both in size and in reputation, winning the respect of parents, employers and the education authorities alike; early statistics collected by HM Inspectors indicated that it was fulfilling its original purpose - that of providing recruits for local industry - admirably: between 1929 and 1933, 90 per cent of the boys who left the School to start work actually did find employment in the engineering and building trades - so there is a very well-founded precedent for the unparalleled graduate employment record which Brunel University enjoys today!

When war broke out the institution - known at this point as Acton Technical College - had to adapt to wartime needs, and during this period it ran an extremely wide range of courses covering everything from basic technical instruction for women and domestic and clerical classes for members of the Women's Services (ATS, WAAF and WRNS), to a degree-level course for engineering cadets. It was immediately after the end of the war that the Government began moves toward a radical restructuring of further education throughout the country, with the objective of improving the nation's skills and ultimately increasing the efficiency of British industry. Each local education authority was required to submit an outline for the provision of further education in its own area, taking into account the views of local industry, neighbouring authorities, universities and voluntary bodies. Middlesex's proposal, which included ambitious plans

Above: The University magazine from 1973. **Below:** *The ultra-modern engineering buildings - 60s style.*

for new buildings and improved facilities, was finally approved in July 1953. In the meanwhile, the Technical College had continued to expand, and now concentrated on the provision of more advanced courses and in particular degree programmes. HM Inspectors who visited in 1952 were extremely impressed by the scope, the appeal and the widespread recognition accorded to the College's range of courses, and concluded that 'the teaching is of a high order and the examination results are excellent'. The only thing which was holding up the College's growth now was the lack of facilities at Acton, and as soon as the Middlesex scheme had received official approval, the institution was able to proceed with the agreed building programme. New buildings on its existing Woodlands site were completed in 1957, and at this point the decision was made to divide the College into two. One establishment retained the name of Acton Technical College and remained in the existing buildings in High Street, where it continued to provide Ordinary National Certificate and craft courses for technicians and craftsmen. The second, which was to be situated in the

new buildings, was to concentrate on the education of technologists, and was named Brunel College of Technology.

Sandwich courses, which were at the time a new concept, had been introduced by the institution the previous year, and Brunel College was a pioneer in this field, concentrating particularly on sandwich courses leading to the Diploma in Technology. The College worked hard to develop a range of courses which suited the needs of local employers, experimenting with various arrangements in order to establish the best model; as a result of this, close links with industry were developed, and this co-operation was to be an integral part of the success of the College in the years to come.

The Government had introduced the designation of College of Advanced Technology in 1956, at which time Acton Technical College, in spite of its high academic

Above: *The buildings in 1968. At this time only a half of the Communal Building was finished.*

standing, had not figured amongst the handful of institutions nominated to become Colleges of Advanced Technology. In 1961 the Ministry of Education conducted a review of further education in Middlesex, as a result of which it expressed the opinion that Brunel College of Technology had 'made a distinguished contribution to the development of advanced technological education' and that the standard of work and quality of staff would in themselves warrant the designation of College of Advanced Technology; however, CATs were expected to be able to accommodate some 2,000 students, and this was clearly well beyond the capacity of the Woodlands site. This signalled the next major step in the institution's development: it was agreed that

plans for further extensions at Woodlands should be abandoned, and instead a completely new college was to be erected on a separate site, as a replacement for the existing college; and the site chosen was a 170-acre plot in Uxbridge. This was formerly the Lowe & Shawyer Nursery and Market Garden. Local historian and Honorary Graduate of the university Ken Pearce records that in its heyday in the 1930s the nursery covered 200 acres, employed over 1,000 people full time and produced around 50 million blooms each year. In fact the Ministry of Education did not wait for the new building to be completed - or even begun - before redesignating the college. With effect from 1st April 1962, the institution officially became Brunel College of Advanced Technology - the tenth of the country's CATs, and in the event the last to achieve this status.

Building at Uxbridge was planned in four phases, with the cost of each phase expected to total around £1.5 million, and Phase One to be substantially completed by June 1967. Then, just two years later, the publication of the Robbins Report announced another far-reaching change for the institution: Brunel College was to become a technological university from 1966, with the power to award its own degrees, both first and higher. The Governing Body and the Academic Board found themselves under pressure from all sides - undertaking academic and financial planning exercises, formulating new policies for the Institution's future as a University, overseeing development of the new site, and at the same time maintaining a high standard of provision for existing students in a climate of impending change.

Left: *The climbing wall at Uxbridge.*
Below: *In July 1999, Brunel awarded an Honorary Degree to one of its most successful alumni, barrister Lincoln Crawford OBE.*

It was inevitable that a number of issues should arise during the course of an undertaking on such a large scale as the construction of an entirely new University. Amendments to the preliminary architects' plans were called for; there was the question of housing for the staff; there was debate over the provision of a generator to provide electricity; there was the matter of bridges across the railway line; and the degree of difficulty experienced in obtaining sufficient funding from the Department of Education made it necessary to scrutinise the financial implications carefully before making any decision. However, one by one all the challenges - whether academic-related, administrative or structural - were met and overcome; the University Charter was granted on 9th June 1966, and from Autumn Term 1966 the Uxbridge campus was officially a part of Brunel University. With the River Pinn meandering across the site, and a tangible link with Brunel the man remaining in a length of cutting from a spur line from his famous Great Western Railway which bisected the land, Uxbridge campus is historically interesting as well as extremely pleasant; indeed, Queen Victoria herself travelled along this particular stretch of railway track on her maiden railway journey, with Daniel Gooch driving, assisted by Mr Brunel himself.

The University continued to operate on the two sites until 1971, when it was finally able to vacate the Acton site which had witnessed the institution's meteoric rise from Junior Technical School to University in less than 40 years. Nineteen seventy-one was also the year in which Dr Topping retired,

and tribute must be paid to the man under whose leadership the institution achieved so much. Appointed Principal of the Technical College in 1955, Dr Topping had remained at the head of the

Below: *Retiring Chancellor, Lord Halsbury (seated) with Brunel's new Chancellor, Lord Wakeham.*
Bottom: *Mill Hall, Uxbridge Campus.*

institution throughout, becoming Vice-Chancellor of the University in 1966.

The Uxbridge campus has of course continued to develop; further investment in careful landscaping and planning over the years has resulted in the pleasant, mature site which we know today, with open lawns, gardens and pathways between the separate faculties, facilities and amenities. One recent addition is the Gaskell Building; named after Elizabeth Gaskell, this building houses the expanding Arts Faculty and part of the Faculty of Social Sciences. Brunel University now operates from four campuses, although Uxbridge remains its administrative centre and main campus. Its campus at Runnymede was formerly the home of Shoreditch College, and became part of the University in 1981; Twickenham and Osterley campuses formed the West London Institute between 1976 and 1995, when they became Brunel University College prior to complete integration into the University in 1997.

At the time of writing Brunel University has over 12,000 students on its four campuses. This student community includes an international student contingent some 1400-strong, drawn from 91 different countries; and all these men and women play an important role in spreading the name of Uxbridge and Brunel throughout the world. Most of them return home as Brunel graduates to practice their professions; and often their recommendation leads other members of their family, friends, colleagues and acquaintances to study at Brunel. The University has a strong support network to ensure that students from overseas settle in quickly and enjoy their time at Uxbridge.

Students participate in a wide variety of music, drama, dance and sporting activities, creating a lively environment where the excellent social and welfare facilities complement the extensive, high quality academic provision. Many courses are designed specifically for students wishing to enter professional and vocational fields, and the course structure is flexible, with a choice of part-time or full-time study, and a range of sandwich and non-sandwich options

available. It is not surprising that Brunel graduates are so highly sought-after by employers, as Brunel has always ensured that its academic syllabus remains relevant to the needs of industry, commerce and the public sector. Undergraduate courses combine academic study with practical work experience, with placements in both industry and the public sector. Brunel graduates are as a rule more mature, more organised, more confident and more useful as a result. Brunel Research is likewise geared to the needs of society. For example, the *ESRC Virtual Society?* programme, now in its third year, is researching the social context of the development and use of new technologies. There are also ground-breaking technological projects in areas such as parallel computing technology, manufacturing metrology and materials processing.

Just as I K Brunel opened up new horizons for the Victorians through his engineering innovations and applications which brought rail travel within their reach, so Brunel University has allowed successive generations to expand their professional and educational horizons, by creating opportunities for students to acquire and apply new knowledge, to explore new areas of research, and to extend the scope of their involvement in the country's industrial and economic future. For more than 30 years, the name of Brunel has been synonymous with the provision high quality academic programmes which meet the needs of the real world and contribute in a very practical way to progress in all walks of life. The story of the creation and development of Brunel University has been one of continual growth while at the same time remaining true to its heritage. We in Uxbridge are proud of the important contributions that this great institution has made in the past, and look forward to a future in which Brunel University continues to play a leading role.

Above: *Relaxing in the campus grounds.*
Below: *All students have the opportunity to work with computers at Brunel.*

At leisure

A sunny September day has attracted children, like bees to a honeypot, to the paddling pool in Uxbridge Recreation Ground, where there is lots of lovely water for wading, paddling - and splashing your sister in the face. Older brothers and sisters watch indulgently, chatting together as the younger members of their families enjoy the cool water and warm sunshine. The attitude of the older children is interesting; it was the norm in the 1930s, when on the whole families were much larger than today, for the older children to take care of their younger siblings. Life was much simpler in those days, and the children pictured here in 1936 will no doubt have played whip and top and hopscotch, and used old tyres for hoops. Their games would have been cowboys and Indians (even the girls!), skipping, hide and seek and catch. Contrast the simple pleasures of old with the TVs and computers which today's children expect!

This page: The weather has to be very warm before you are brave enough to go swimming at the open air pool, but there have always been some intrepid souls who would defy the British weather to don their swimming costumes and risk a few goose pimples. Unfortunately, we have no date for these scenes, but though the day looks quite pleasant there are still more people hanging around the margins of the pool than there are swimming in the water! Built at a cost of £24,500, the pool was opened on 31st August 1935, and a huge crowd packed into the stands to attend the opening ceremony. This was a red letter day for the town, as before this the swimmers of Uxbridge only had a bathing area on the Frays to practise their skills. The 220ft pool was an important addition to the town, and competitors in the 1948 Olympic Games (based at RAF Uxbridge, which acted as the Olympic village) used it for their training.

The style of swimwear has changed more than a little since the pool was first built; back then many men still sported all-in-one costumes with shoulder-straps, and although the odd two-piece costume could be seen among the ladies (very daring), bikinis were undreamed of at the time. It was 1946 when the skimpy costumes were created by French designer Louis Reard, and the daring new swimwear that revealed flesh hitherto unseen in public was immediately labelled indecent and immodest....If they could only see us now! Swimming caps (usually made of white rubber and with an uncomfortable strap that fastened under the chin), were customary among the ladies, and remained popular until recent years. Today, their use seems to have been abandoned -not only because they were labelled naff by trendy young girls, but because they never did keep out the water anyway! Was it during the 1960s that coloured flowers (rubber of course!) were added to brighten up the ugly caps?

The outdoor pool remains just as popular with today's families, and still opens during the summer months from May to September.

Right: This cookery class took place at Greenway School, and the average age of the students leads us to conclude that this was an evening class. The group consisted mostly of ladies, as at the time of the photograph a woman's place was very definitely in the kitchen - though we can see that a couple of young men are braving the scorn of their peer group! Christmas is obviously approaching, and the tutor, whose name has unfortunately disappeared in the mists of time, is demonstrating to the class the use of the icing syringe. (How many readers remember those clever tubes with a plunger to force the icing through the nozzle?) Nylon icing bags were still far in the future. On the blackboard behind the students, a recipe for almond icing has been written up; was this from a week or two back, we wonder? The class has now moved on to the royal icing stage, and from there to adding the final decorations -complete, we take it, with the compulsory miniature Santa Claus, Christmas tree and foil frill.

Below: This photograph raises more questions than it answers, the first one being not What? but Why? The reason these young lads were being taught the art of net making is not clear, though some of them perhaps went on to manufacture a comfortable hammock as a Christmas present for Mum or Dad. The perfect gift for the man or woman who has everything? This would have been a soothing craft to learn, creating strips of netting with wooden netting needles and measures - and making the odd slip knot instead of the required herring knot! This was May 1933, and one or two of our more mature readers may be able to look back and recall acquiring the craft of netting while they were pupils at Uxbridge Senior School. From so many years on many of us tend to look back on the 1930s as a time when school lessons held nothing more exciting than the three 'R's, but we can see from this photograph that arts and crafts figured highly on the school curriculum. Displayed on the wall behind are examples of calligraphy, painting and collage - a credit to the art teacher, whoever he or she was.

Events of the 1940s

MELODY MAKERS
The songs of radio personalities such as Bing Crosby and Vera Lynn were whistled, sung and hummed everywhere during the 1940s. The 'forces' sweetheart' brought hope to war-torn Britain with 'When the Lights go on Again', while the popular crooner's 'White Christmas' is still played around Christmas time even today. Who can forget songs like 'People Will Say we're in Love', 'Don't Fence Me In', 'Zip-a-dee-doo-dah', and 'Riders in the Sky'?

INVENTION AND TECHNOLOGY
Inspired by quick-drying printers' ink, in 1945 Hungarian journalist Laszlo Biro developed a ballpoint pen which released viscous ink from its own reservoir as the writer moved the pen across the page. An American inventor was working on a similar idea at the same time, but it was Biro's name that stuck. A few years later Baron Bich developed a low cost version of the pen, and the 'Bic' ballpoint went on sale in France in 1953.

SCIENCE AND DISCOVERY
In 1943 Ukrainian-born biochemist Selman Abraham Waksman made a significant discovery. While studying organisms found in soil he discovered an antibiotic (a name Waksman himself coined) which was later found to be the very first effective treatment for tuberculosis. A major killer for thousands of years, even the writings of the ancient Egyptians contain stories of people suffering from tuberculosis. Waksman's development of streptomycin brought him the 1952 Nobel Prize for Medicine.

School swimming classes had been cancelled when this photograph was taken, and a land drill of swimming movements, demonstrated here by Helen Yates, was as good as it appears to have got. Having learnt the necessary strokes and watched them being put into practice by experts, the children were expected to visit the pool and learn to swim in their own time. How many of them actually learned to keep

their feet off the bottom by using this unique method of coaching, we wonder? The out of school class appears to have been popular with the boys and girls, however, and they are watching the demonstrator's progress with real interest. We note that they are all dressed in swimwear, and with their hopes high for their own success in acquiring the crawl, were ready and waiting to jump into the water to follow suit.

Helen Yates was doing her level best to pass on a skill which might at some time in the future save a life. At the time, Helen (who was in the WRNS service) was the English 220 yards champion.

'Patronised by Royalty' reads the rather untidy sign attached to the clairvoyant's makeshift booth to the left of this photograph, taken at the Uxbridge Show in 1935, *(above)* and 'In your dreams,' we would be tempted to comment.... A willing child dressed appropriately and stood in the booth to advertise the fortune teller's services. But who, at the Uxbridge Show on this beautiful day, would be at all concerned with the supernatural and the unknown future? It was the present day that was important to these young competitors who had brought their beloved pets to try their luck in the Show. Which of them won, we wonder? Dressing up was all part of the day's fun, and one little girl has decided to wow the judges with her gorgeous Christmas tree fairy costume.

The Uxbridge Show featured large in the calendar of local people, whether they were competing in the driving events, showing their dogs, or baking fruit cakes, but the Show as it was in 1935 bore no resemblance to the small horticultural event it had grown from. Originally staged back in 1909 to display the green-fingered talents of the Uxbridge and District Horticultural Society, the occasion proved popular and developed into an annual event that grew year by year as new events were introduced. By the mid 1930s, the clouds of war were beginning to gather on the horizon and just before war was declared in 1939 the Show attracted a massive crowd of 13,000. With the creation of the new Borough in 1965 the event became known as the Hillingdon Show, and it remains a popular day of family fun today.

Events & occasions

What a marvellous sight this parade must have been as, following each other closely, a long line of imaginative floats made their way slowly along the High Street. This procession formed part of the celebrations that marked the Silver Jubilee of King George V and Queen Mary, and thousands of people turned out to line the route of the procession. Children crowded to the front where they could get a better view of what was going on, or were lifted up by Mum or Dad to marvel at the intricate costumes and ingenious tableaux that had been put together. The organisers would have been working on the costumes and props for weeks if not months beforehand.

George Duke of York came to the throne in 1910. The model of the ideal Englishman, King George V had made himself immensely popular with his subjects without really trying. He was tolerant of people whose opinions differed from his own - but not afraid to speak his mind when the occasion called for straight talking. Dignified, fair, conscientious and modest, he once remarked on the warmth with which people greeted him during his Silver Jubilee celebrations, 'I am beginning to think they like me for myself.' George V was the first monarch to broadcast a Christmas Day message over the radio; the Christmas Broadcast became the established tradition that we still enjoy today. When he died in 1936, King George V was genuinely mourned by the whole nation. His widow, Queen Mary, lived on until 1953.

Above: They might not have won an Olympic gold medal, but these boys were justifiably proud of their sporting achievements as, watched by their parents, they queued to receive their well-deserved trophy on school Sports Day, 29th June 1933. Sports Day was a day of fun and challenge that was looked forward to for months, and in every school around Uxbridge children would have been training for many weeks in advance. First of all would come the fun events that involved forfeits and obstacles. How many readers remember their struggles to remain upright and on their feet in the sack race, or to keep a rather large egg from falling out of a spoon? Those were the days! Then there would be the serious events that really sorted the sheep from the goats. The hundred yards dash, the relay race, the high jump, the long jump - all would have been there, and all helping to keep the children fit and healthy.

Right: Some of us love it, others hate it, but either way the 'white stuff' is something we just have to learn to live with, though strangely we seem to have experienced far fewer heavy snowfalls in recent years. Hard at work and armed with a shovel apiece, these hard-working snow shifters would probably agree that snow is delightful on Christmas cards, but much less welcome underfoot! This winter wonderland was Park Road - quite a different place when the photographer recorded this scene for posterity. Not a car was in sight - not even a solitary vehicle abandoned to the drifting snow - and it is hard to relate this almost rural view with today's busy main road to the M40! The intervening years have added a long wall to separate the RAF station (which was established in the town back in 1917, when the service was still the Royal Flying Corps) from the rest of humankind.

The High Street had been turned into a wonderland of red, white and blue when these fascinating images were caught by the photographer. It is unfortunate that these two pictures are undated, but the fashions worn by passers-by, along with the vehicles, lead us to believe that the event being celebrated was the coronation of King George VI in 1937. Prince Albert had been hurled unexpectedly into the kingship he had not been trained for when Edward VIII, his older brother, who was king for a mere 325 days, renounced the throne on 10th December 1936 for American divorcee Wallis Simpson, 'the woman I love'. Edward, dubbed 'the Society Prince', had been well-liked for his natural charm, and many must have hoped that he would be allowed to marry the woman he loved. But Wallis Simpson had been divorced twice, the King was Head of the Church of England - and the Church's teaching on divorce was clear. Edward went the way his heart dictated, and he signed the Instrument of Abdication on the 10th December 1936. The document was witnessed by his three brothers. The new king, George VI, was shy and nervous and suffered from an embarrassing stammer (which he later overcame with medical aid and the support of his wife Queen Elizabeth). 'I'm only a naval officer,' he confessed to his cousin Lord Louis Mountbatten on the day he became king. 'It's the only thing I know about.' He had never seen a state paper in his life. But with typical courage he rose to the challenge, squared his shoulders, and adopted the title of George VI. King George VI went on to take his place as perhaps Britain's most well loved monarch.

Events of the 1950s

WHAT'S ON?

Television hit Britain in a big way during the 1950s. Older readers will surely remember 'Double Your Money, Dixon of Dock Green and 'Dragnet' (whose characters' names were changed 'to protect the innocent'). Commercial television was introduced on 22nd September 1955, and Gibbs SR toothpaste were drawn out of the hat to become the first advert to be shown. Many believed adverts to be vulgar, however, and audiences were far less than had been hoped for.

GETTING AROUND

The year 1959 saw the development of the world's first practical air-cushion vehicle - better known to us as the hovercraft. The earliest model was only able to travel at slow speeds over very calm water and was unable to carry more than three passengers. The faster and smoother alternative to the sea ferry quickly caught on, and by the 1970s a 170-ton car-carrying hovercraft service had been introduced across the English Channel.

SPORTING CHANCE

The four-minute mile had remained the record since 1945, and had become regarded as virtually unbreakable. On 6th May 1954, however, Oxford University student Roger Bannister literally ran away with the record, accomplishing the seemingly impossible in three minutes 59.4 seconds. Bannister collapsed at the end of his last amazing lap, even temporarily losing his vision. By the end of the day, however, he had recovered sufficiently to celebrate his achievement in a London night club!

While for some the 1920s were 'roaring', for others they were years of national depression and long-lasting unemployment. Servicemen who had returned home disabled in 1918 at the end of the first world war faced a future of unemployment and the prospect of living on a pittance, and as the decade progressed things went from bad to worse. In 1928 a national Unemployment Fund was

created - the 'dole' of a pitiful sum that was barely enough to keep alive on, yet incredibly many well-to-do citizens found the dole infuriating. Ignoring the disabilities that prevented many from working in traditional jobs, they viewed the benefit as encouraging laziness. The 1930s remained grim for the unemployed. In 1931, the meagre unemployment benefits were cut by ten per cent and the hated 'Means Test' was introduced to examine the personal circumstances of those applying for aid. This photograph was taken to mark the protest made in October 1936, when men and women who had lost their sight marched through the streets to campaign for better treatment.

Pages 60 - 65: Uxbridge has been home to the Royal Air Force since the early days of flying. Back in 1917 the Royal Flying Corps, as they were until the following year, moved into the Hillingdon House Estate and established the Armament and Gunnery School there. Most people will have heard about T E Lawrence - known popularly as Lawrence of Arabia - and his connection with the town. Lawrence, who worked for British intelligence during World War I, became discontented with British policy in the Middle East and in 1922 he sought obscurity in the RAF, enlisting under the name of Ross. He was killed in a

Events of the 1950s

HOT OFF THE PRESS
The 1950s seemed to be the heyday of spies, and in 1951 the activities of Guy Burgess and Donald Maclean caused a sensation in the country. Both had occupied prominent positions in the Foreign Office, while Burgess had also been a member of MI-6. Recruited by the Russians while at Cambridge University in the 1930s, the traitors provided the Soviets with a huge amount of valuable information. They disappeared in 1951, surfacing in Moscow five years later.

THE WORLD AT LARGE
Plans to develop the economies of member states into one common market came to fruition on 1st January 1958, when the EEC came into operation. The original members were France, Belgium, Luxembourg, The Netherlands, Italy, and West Germany. The Community became highly successful, achieving increased trade and prosperity across Western Europe while at the same time alleviating fear of war which lingered on after the end of World War II. Britain became a member in 1973.

SCIENCE AND DISCOVERY
DNA (deoxyribonucleic acid) was first defined as long ago as 1953, and the effects have been far-reaching. The key discovery was developed over the following years and today DNA fingerprinting has become an accepted part of life. Genetic diseases such as hemophilia and cystic fibrosis have been identified. Criminals are continually detected and brought to justice. Biological drugs have been developed. More controversially, drought and disease-resistant plants have been engineered - and Dolly the sheep has been produced.

motorcycle accident in 1935.

It was 1920 when the prestigious RAF Central Band came to Uxbridge, and the town had - and still has - every right to take pride in 'their' band. The band was central to the celebrations in 1960 that marked the presentation of the freedom of entry into the borough to RAF Uxbridge, and though we have no date for this collection of

Events of the 1950s

MELODY MAKERS
Few teenage girls could resist the blatant sex-appeal of 'Elvis the Pelvis', though their parents were scandalised at the moody Presley's provocatively gyrating hips. The singer took America and Britain by storm with such hits as 'Jailhouse Rock', 'All Shook Up' and 'Blue Suede Shoes'. The rhythms of Bill Haley and his Comets, Buddy Holly, Chuck Berry, and Roy Orbison (who had a phenomenal three-octave voice) turned the 1950s into the Rock 'n' Roll years.

INVENTION AND TECHNOLOGY
Until the late 1950s you did not carry radios around with you. Radios were listened to at home, plugged into a mains socket in every average sitting room. Japan was in the forefront of electronic developments even then, and in 1957 the Japanese company Sony introduced the world's very first all-transistor radio - an item of new technology that was small enough to fit into your pocket. The major consumer product caught on fast - particularly with teenage listeners.

ROYAL WATCH
King George VI's health had been causing problems since 1948, when he developed thrombosis. In 1951 the King - always a heavy smoker - became ill again, and was eventually found to be suffering from lung cancer. His left lung was removed in September of 1951. In January 1952 he waved Princess Elizabeth and Prince Philip off on their tour of Africa; they were never to see him again. The King died on 5th February 1952

photographs, they could have been taken to mark this special occasion. The freedom of entry gave the RAF station the right to march through the streets of Uxbridge on all ceremonial occasions with drums, bands and flying colours - not to mention drawn swords and fixed bayonets! As today's youngsters would say - cool!

The band, which still insists on a high standard of musicianship from its members, today has around 42 members, who are encouraged to become involved in other kinds of musical activity. In earlier years this meant the involvement of band members in the RAF Symphony Orchestra. State visits, the Edinburgh Military Tattoo, changing the guard at Buckingham Palace, and many more events including the recording of music produced on cassette and CD are now a regular part of the life of the band.

Everyone loves a parade, especially if there is a rousing band to keep everyone in step, and Uxbridge has long known about rousing bands.... It was August 1938 when this particular parade made its way through the streets of the town, and though we can not be sure what occasion was being celebrated the event brought out the local people in full force. What fun these children are having as they rush to the head of the procession to keep step with the band! Britain was still at peace at the time, but preparations for war were already going ahead,

with the building of the underground Operations Centre at RAF Uxbridge, from where the Battle of Britain was coordinated.

September 1939 saw the outbreak of World War II, when across the country military parades became an accepted part of life. Children loved the excitement of the stirring music, the beat of the drum and the marching military men, every one in step. Parades were important, too, for morale, as they undoubtedly made the average person in the street feel in touch with the military and the progress of the war.

Above: *It is Charter Day, 1955, and the crowds are out in full force, from Grandma and Auntie Flo to the latest babe in arms. In the High Street, bunting has been strung from pole to pole, and patriotic flags flap gaily in the breeze. The Regal Cinema - the venue for the event - has been glorified with colourful banners, flower displays and greenery - and the red carpet is in place across the pavement for the benefit of The Duchess of Kent. The Duchess was here to perform the pleasant duty of presenting Uxbridge with its charter, and the photograph shows her emerging from the cinema after the ceremony. Representatives from RAF Uxbridge stand smartly to attention.*

The growing town had waited four years to see this day, and civic pride was running high among the local people. It was back in 1951 when the Uxbridge Urban District Council petitioned for borough status. Now the long-awaited charter had been granted, and it was time to let the flags fly. Further developments were to follow with the reorganisation of London in 1973, when 32 new boroughs were created and Uxbridge became the town centre for Hillingdon.

The TV cop chats amicably with officers from the real life version at the Hillingdon Show in 1966. Frank Windsor is one of the guests, pictured here with Robert Keegan and the representatives of law and order. The popularity of 'Z-Cars' will be well remembered by 'cops and robbers' enthusiasts. The long-running police drama series strangely enough owed its origins to a bout of mumps. To pass the time writer Troy Kennedy Martin, confined to bed and feeling very fed up with life, tuned in to the police waveband, and discovered a whole new world that was nothing like

'Z-Cars' introduced a completely different type of police drama to the British public

the comfy 'Dixon of Dock Green' type of policing portrayed on television. He took up a pen and began to write, and the result was a completely different type of police drama that even had a nasty and aggressive superior officer, Charlie Barlow, played by Stratford Johns. In fact Martin's characters were all fallible human beings who had their own personal vices. The series, which portrayed the real relationship between police and the community, kicked off in 1962 on BBC 1 and immediately gained a huge following.

On the move

This page: A sight to bring back memories to the few who remember the rattle and sway of the old trams *(below).* This Number 7 Feltham-type car stands at the tramway terminus, and we can see that as cars approach the end of the line, the double track becomes a single. As the tram moves off again in the opposite direction, spring points will change, automatically shunting the vehicle on to the other set of lines. Very ingenious.

London's last trams were made in 1931, though trams ran in Uxbridge for a further five years. When the service came to an end, the most recent cars were still in good condition and were sold on; some of the fleet were acquired by Leeds, while others went even further north to Sunderland. Happily, one of these was installed at Crich tramway museum in Derbyshire and restored to its full glory.

In virtually the same spot stands one of the new breed of vehicles - trolley buses - which replaced Uxbridge's trams in 1936 *(bottom).* The change-over was made in response to the growing traffic levels in the town centre. While the trolley buses were, of course, still confined by a set of overhead lines, at least the new service freed up the centre of the road to traffic. Tram lines are still in place at the time of the photograph, so the scene was captured soon after the change-over, and Uxbridge along with towns up and down the country were left with the problem of what to do with the old lines! Some, with an eye to the scrap value, dug them up, while others simply spread tarmac over them.

Both pictures: Where did they all go to? Police officers on point duty, that is. There was a time when every major junction in every major town had its traffic 'bobby'; remember those black and white zebra-striped boxes they used to use? A few at a time they departed, leaving the motorist with a legacy of traffic lights to contend with *(above)*. The names above the shops may have changed since the photographer captured this scene, but all the same this is a view which will be instantly recognised by every reader. The Piccadilly Underground line began to run through to Uxbridge in 1933, and the increased traffic taxed Belmont Road station to its limits. The 'new' Metropolitan and Piccadilly Line station that we know today was opened in 1938; those were the days when slum clearance was making a clean sweep many of the yards that led off the High Street, and the station replaced the old Bell Yard. We can thank Charles Holden, the designer, for the elegant sweep of the new building, while Erwin Bossanyi's fine stained glass windows added the finishing touch to the spacious interior.

Boots eventually took over the Timothy Whites chain, whose name still carried 'and Taylors' at the time of the photograph, and their store today trades from the same position near the station entrance - handy for that lunchtime sandwich!

Traffic congestion was an accepted part of life in Uxbridge by the 1930s. Uxbridge was expanding rapidly, with new industry attracting people to settle here and a large number of middle-class houses being built to accommodate them. With the town's growth came the motor car, that badge of increasing prosperity, and in consequence the High Street was often choked with cars, delivery wagons and trams. In 1936 Uxbridge's trams were replaced by trolley buses in an attempt to address the problem. Car 303, on the Number 7 route to Shepherds Bush, sports the commonly-seen prominent red triangle, which was placed on the front of trams to warn passing motorists that passengers would be alighting in the middle of the road.

This particular sign was unlikely to have been illuminated, as the later ones were (revealing the words

Events of the 1960s

MELODY MAKERS

The 1960s: those were the days when the talented blues guitarist Jimi Hendrix shot to rock stardom, a youthful Cliff Richard charmed the nation with his 'Congratulations' and Sandie Shaw won the Eurovision Song Contest for Britain with 'Puppet on a String'. It was the combined musical talents of a group of outrageous working-class Liverpool lads, however, who formed the Beatles and took the world by storm with music that ranged from the experimental to ballads such as 'Yesterday'.

INVENTION AND TECHNOLOGY

A major step forward was made in 1960 when the laser was invented. An acronym for Light Amplification by Stimulated Emission of Radiation, the device produces a narrow beam of light that can travel for vast distances and is focused to give enormous power. Laser beams, as well as being able to carry far more information than radio waves, can also be used for surgery, cutting, drilling, welding and scores of other operations.

SCIENCE AND DISCOVERY

When the drug Thalidomide was first developed during the 1950s it was hailed as a wonder drug which would ease the distressing symptoms of pregnancy sickness. By the early 1960s the drug's terrible side effects were being discovered, when more than 3000 babies had been born with severe birth defects. Malformed limbs, defective eyes and faulty intestines were the heart-rending legacy left by Thalidomide.

'Westinghouse air brake'). The busy and popular Kings Arms pub, on the left of the photograph, was AA registered and offered car parking facilities as well as tasty luncheons and suppers. How much did lunch at the Kings Arms cost at the time, we wonder? Few will today recall the old arcade which once stood on the opposite side of the High Street, replaced long ago by a succession of shops. The Chimes shopping development was by the end of the 1990s set to take the place of many of the buildings on the right.

With his back to the oncoming tram and standing just inches away from the rail, this man (who would appear by his cap to be an official of some kind) seems about to be sandwiched between the two vehicles. If this should turn out to be his unlucky day, all was not lost as the trams were all fitted with safety rails, known to most as 'dog catchers'. This clever innovation would have swept dropped parcels, dogs - and the odd human - away from the tram's wheels, so we have grounds for believing that he did not end up as a part of the town's accident statistics!

Of interest to the left of the photograph is the

charabanc (was it a Leyland?) standing at the kerbside outside Waddington's jeweller's. Many of the 'charas' served a dual purpose; during the week they acted as delivery vehicles, then when the weekend came, rows of seats were added ready for those trips to the seaside that became popular with office and shop workers during the 1920s and 30s. The trips offered a great day out at a reasonable price, and once the charabanc was bowling along the sun and wind would blow any workaday blues away. The vehicle was convertible, and in the event of rain the fold-down hood would be hastily fixed in place.

Above: Not only a work of art but a display of great skill, and the proud, green-fingered station master poses proudly alongside what we can suppose is his own creation. How many hours did he spend pricking out all these tiny blooms, then nurturing them and keeping the bed free of weeds as the flowers grew to form the words? This is certainly one photograph which we would appreciate viewing in colour! The High Street Station was opened in May 1907 by the Great Western Railway virtually opposite the Treaty House, and its position on the embankment, accessed by a long stairway, gave it a pigeon's eye view across the Uxbridge rooftops. The High Street was the GWR's second station in the town - Vine Street had been opened in the early days of the railway back in 1856. Plans were drawn up to link the two stations, and the company even acquired some of the land that would be needed. When war broke out in 1914 the plans were shelved and in the event the link was never built. Uxbridge High Street station was closed to passengers at the beginning of World War II and though it continued to carry goods traffic for many years it never reopened as a passenger line. Both GWR branch lines closed in the mid 1960s.

Right: A couple of buses and the nearby railway lines give the only clue to the exact location of this view of Uxbridge, which has changed beyond all recognition since this photograph was taken in 1950. Younger readers in particular will struggle to conjure up in their imagination the bus station and garage and the tall office blocks which now stand on what was at one time open land. Building work was already taking place, and a group of workers contemplate their progress amid piles of bricks, scaffolding, machinery and all the other paraphernalia that are part and parcel of every building site. In the late 1970s work began on the new bus station, which was opened in 1983. What a pity that its over-tight turning circle (which calls for real skill from local bus drivers) could not have been considered at the initial planning stage! Bus stations and railway stations go together like cheese and wine - but it is surprising how many towns have separated these two means of transport by a ten minute walk. Fine for taxi drivers, though not good for holiday-makers carrying heavy suitcases and wheeling a baby buggy! Uxbridge, however, is different, and travellers arriving by train have only to walk a few yards to catch their bus home - so sensible!

Many readers will remember the war memorial when it was situated outside the St Andrew's gate of the RAF camp, and in this view from January 1958 we can see that wreaths have been laid at the foot of the memorial. The sleek Saab turning at the junction is the only moving vehicle in the scene, but as the decade progressed the volume of traffic in the town swelled.

Uxbridge decided on a programme of redevelopment, and in 1972 the cenotaph was moved to its present position in the old burial ground.

When Lady Hillingdon unveiled the memorial in 1924 people firmly believed that the 'war to end all wars' had already been fought - it was unthinkable that such misery and distress should ever be gone through again,

and the words 'Erected in honour and in memory of all those men and women of Uxbridge who served or fell in the Great War 1914 - 1918' formed part of the legend on the plinth. They had no way of knowing that the future held yet more suffering and loss for Uxbridge, and the words 'In Memoriam 1939 - 1945' were later added to the cenotaph.

Events of the 1960s

WHAT'S ON?

Television comedy came into its own in the 1960s, and many of the shows that were favourites then went on to become classics. 'On the Buses', 'Steptoe and Son', 'Till Death Us Do Part' and 'The Army Game' kept audiences laughing, while the incredible talents of Morecambe and Wise, the wit of Des O'Connor - often the butt of the duo's jokes - and the antics of Benny Hill established them for ever in the nation's affections.

GETTING AROUND

The 2nd March 1969 was a landmark in the history of aviation. The Anglo-French supersonic airliner Concorde took off for the first time from Toulouse in France. Concorde, which can cruise at almost twice the speed of sound, was designed to fly from London to New York in an incredible three hours twenty minutes. The event took place just weeks after the Boeing 747, which can carry 500 passengers to Concorde's modest 100, made its first flight.

SPORTING CHANCE

Wembley Stadium saw scenes of jubilation when on 30th July 1966 England beat West Germany 4-2 in the World Cup. The match, played in a mixture of sunshine and showers, had been a nailbiting experience for players and spectators alike from the very beginning when Germany scored only thirteen minutes into the game. It was Geoff Hurst's two dramatic goals scored in extra time that secured the victory and lifted the cup for England - at last.

Events of the 1960s

HOT OFF THE PRESS

Barbed wire, concrete blocks and a wide no-man's-land divided East from West when a reinforced wall was built right across the city of Berlin in 1961. Many East Germans escaped to the West at the eleventh hour, taking with them only the possessions they could carry. The Berlin Wall divided the city - and hundreds of family members and friends - for 28 years until the collapse of Communist rule across Eastern Europe. Who can ever forget those scenes in 1989, when ordinary people themselves began to physically tear down the hated wall?

THE WORLD AT LARGE

'One giant leap for mankind' was taken on 20th July 1969, when Neil Armstrong made history as the first man to set foot on the moon. During the mission he and fellow-astronaut 'Buzz' Aldrin collected rock and soil samples, conducted scientific experiments - and had a lot of fun jumping around in the one-sixth gravity. Twenty-one hours and thirty-seven minutes after their landing they took off again in their lunar module 'Eagle' to rejoin Apollo II which was orbiting above them, proudly leaving the American flag on the Moon's surface.

ROYAL WATCH

Princess Margaret's announcement in 1960 that she was to wed photographer Antony Armstrong-Jones (later Lord Snowdon) brought sighs of relief from her immediate family. Just five years earlier the people of Britain had sympathised as the princess bowed to public and private pressure, ending her relationship with Peter Townsend, Prince Philip's former equerry. The Church (and the Queen, as its Head) frowned on the liaison as Townsend was divorced. Her marriage to Lord Snowdon itself ended in 1978.

Both pictures: This driver of a trolley bus on the 607 route replaces the booms after passing another vehicle at the terminus at the bottom of the High Street; an awkward job at the best of times *(main picture)*. Has his colleague perhaps broken down? We will never know. The 607 route that ran between Uxbridge and Shepherds Bush was introduced in November 1936, replacing the old tram service. Buses have long been regarded as very convenient mobile advertisement hoardings, but the message seen here on a 607 trolley bus (and appearing on quite a number of the

fleet back in 1960, the year of the photograph) is rather enigmatic. The words Where? Here! obviously drove home an important message to passers by and passengers at the time *(inset)*. It was 9th November 1960 when the last 607 trolley buses were replaced by diesel buses; at the same time the powers that be changed the route number to 207. Transport enthusiasts - and there are many of them around - will have recognised that this vehicle has a British United Traction chassis.

In the 1960s, the roar of the diesel bus replaced the quiet purr of the smooth-running trolley buses, though their traction poles stayed put, reminding us of the old 'trackless trams' for almost 20 years. They were eventually removed in 1981. Trolley buses ran in various places around the country until the 1970s, and on Sunday 26th March 1972 vehicle number 844 - part of Bradford, West Yorkshire's, fleet - was chosen to become Britain's very last trolley bus.

Shopping spree

Familiar - yet unfamiliar. This was Uxbridge when it opened in 1933 as the 'Main Market', and Thursday 2nd November was the grand opening day of this fine facility. Major E W C Flavell was to do the honours on the big day, and the banner over the entrance also tells us that cash prizes were being offered. What a pity that we cannot find out, so many years on, how competitors could win the prizes, and who were the lucky winners! Uxbridge High Street itself had an exciting mix of shops and services; for example, on either side of the arcade entrance were a tobacconist and a sweet shop (where 6d would buy you half a pound of Cadbury's Bournville chocolate!). No shades of wartime rationing here. The adjoining filling station to the left offered local motorists Shell petrol or Ethyl; wasn't Ethyl an alcohol based fuel?

The arcade was modernised during the 1960s and remains today. It may be small, but whether you are looking for a fashionable blouse, a pattern for a doll's outfit, a pair of dance shoes from pink ballet to Irish 'Riverdance' style, a cat collar or a copy of the 'Daily Telegraph', today's arcade is where you are likely to find them - before relaxing over a quick coffee at Granny Satchwill's!

Below: Tom Thompson was just 16, and new to the family business when this photograph was taken in the mid 1930s. The greater part of this marvellous window display was taken up with sweets and tobacco, though as far as we can gather, model railways were already an important side of the business. From the moment he was given his first train set as a small boy Tom was hooked, and he was to see the model railway side of the business develop and eventually take over completely from cigarettes and confectionery. Over the years he built up an in-depth knowledge of anything that ran on parallel lines, and among the clients who came to consult him were technicians from Pinewood Studios and physicists from Brunel University. In 1983 Tom decided that the shop had reached the end of the line - though retirement for him simply meant that he would be able to give time to his lifelong hobby. Having passed his tram driver's test in 1979, he would spend more time driving trams at the museum at Crich, Derbyshire, and the locomotive at Ruislip Lido.

Right: 'Entire premises coming down! All stock must be cleared!' shout the signs announcing Mulhollands rebuilding sale, though there are few passers by to take note of the attractive offers. Two or three young mothers have paused to examine the extensive range of shoes in the window; did they go home that day with a new pair for their toddlers? The rebuilding work was carried out in 1936, and the old building was to lose its little dormer windows, its flowing lettering and its pelmet of homely curtaining, and though many readers will be familiar with Mulhollands, few will remember the shop before the major facelift. The adjoining business, E E Chaney's, bakers, had had a presence in Uxbridge for many years, borne out by the notice by the door: ' Estd over 100 years'. Chaney's carried the well known Hovis sign high on their building. Interestingly, the name Hovis (the winner of a competition to decide on a name for the bread) is a contraction of the Latin 'hominus vis' - 'the strength of man'.

The thick blackout blinds in place in some of these King's Parade shop windows are grim reminders that this was wartime Uxbridge. The month was October, and the darker early evenings would call for lights to be lit and blinds to be in place, so it is not too clear which of the shops is open and which have closed for the day! Product displays and advertising boards are still in place outside Critchley's Woolclean, enabling us to discover (or remember, according to our age!) that for the princely sum of two shillings (ten new pence) you could have a lady's costume or a

During the war, children across the country had to make do with eating cocoa powder mixed with a spoonful of sugar

gent's suit cleaned. This was obviously also a sweets and tobacco shop, though confectionery was strictly rationed during the second world war. When there were no sweets to be had, children across the country were reduced to eating cocoa powder with a spoonful of precious sugar in a screw of paper, or even a 'penny Oxo' for an occasional savoury treat. Players cigarettes - also advertised on a pavement board - have been pleasing smokers since the enduring slogan 'Players Please' appeared back in the 1920s. Remember the rather romantic Players Navy Cut sailor on their early adverts?

At work

Before the development of the High Street began, there were many little alleys and yards such as Bell Yard, pictured here in August 1932. At the time of the photograph Bell Yard was a thriving and close-knit community, and the group of children captured by the photographer were happy enough to be playing together with their carts and old prams, though one little girl was lucky enough to own a bike! Were they contemplating calling in at Percy's shop to buy one of the tempting ice creams advertised on a board outside, we wonder? At the time, Percy's was undergoing extensive alterations, and though a number of prominent notices tell passers-by that business was 'as usual' we can't help concluding that such large scale renovations would severely disrupt the store's day to day trading!

Many of Uxbridge's overcrowded and insanitary yards were demolished during the 1930s. The old rows of small cottages boasted few refinements, and residents were used to doing without bathrooms and using outside toilets. It would have been an exciting day when they were at last able to move to the new council estates, where they had hot and cold running water and electricity, for which they had waited so long.

Pavilions of splendour - from High Street to high style

In the space of just forty years, shopping in Uxbridge has been transformed from a traditional High Street to a contemporary covered shopping centre.

Not every step of the journey has been painless, but the end results have created a shopping environment which is covered, comfortable and convenient, while still enjoying a personality and ambience unique to the town.

Like so many places, Uxbridge endured the wholesale and unsympathetic redevelopment of the town centre in the 1970s when the traditional High Street was demolished to make way for a 70s concrete carbuncle.

An imaginative refurbishment of the scheme in the mid-80s however, has revitalised the town by both covering the pedestrian malls and providing a variety of interesting architectural features - like the imposing Market Tower and the quirky sculpted figures that have been happily playing croquet and watering the glass on the roofs of the market shops.

Unlike so many modern centres, the Pavilions enjoys features that reflect the heritage of the site with its market stalls and shops.

Over the last fifteen years, the Pavilions has not only proved popular with shoppers but also with shops and stores attracting many of the best and newest names in retailing to the town.

There are seldom empty units within the scheme and those that do become available are quickly snapped up by businesses keen to capitalise on the large number of regular visitors from the prosperous residential areas that surround Uxbridge.

This page: *Buildings in the old Uxbridge High Street prior to the construction of the original 1970s precinct.*

The shopping centre and its traders are by no means complacent about their position in the marketplace and regular research has been used to review further improvements that have been implemented over the last fifteen years.

A series of marketing initiatives have also been undertaken, which have on four occasions, been recognised in Marketing Excellence Awards from the British Council of Shopping Centre and International Council of Shopping Centres.

The Centre's owners and the Merchants Association representing stores within the Centre, are always looking for new ways to satisfy the public's demands for a shopping centre and a focus for the community.

As active participants within the town centre initiative the Pavilions is also instrumental in working to improve every element of life in the town centre from public transport to parking to shopping and leisure.

This page: *Draughty, cold and wet' was the verdict of one shopper who recalls the High Street shopping centre as it used to be - an opinion no doubt echoed among many locals who struggled with dripping umbrellas, cutting winds and awkward pushchairs back in the 1970s! Interestingly, the brochure for the original shopping centre read '...a feature of the development is an open market entirely covered by an attractive glazed canopy to ensure comfortable shopping in all weathers.' The intention was there, but unfortunatley the reality of the 'attractive glazed canopy' never came about, and shopping remained less than pleasant until the dramatic transformation of the facility that began in the 1980s.*

Above: Crowds gather in the Market Square for the official launch of Christmas. This annual event attracts crowds of over 5,000 who enjoy a Parade through the High Street with Santa, Bands, Clowns, Jugglers and a sleigh pulled by real reindeer from the Cairngorm Reindeer Centre after which the Market Place becomes an ideal arena for family entertainment and a Christmas sing song and get together.

Over the years, a whole host of acts have participated within Christmas Launches, Fashion Shows, Carol Concerts and Charity functions including Rolf Harris, Barbara Windsor, Roy Castle, Paul Daniels, Henry Cooper, Gospel Choirs, World Pro Yo-Yo Champion, Power Rangers, Spice Girls Tribute Band and the Bishop of London

The annual modelling competition run by the Centre generates up to 500 entrants and the Centre's own Children's Club hosted by Pavilions mascot, Dandy the Lion, has over 1,000 members.

helpful security officers'...'Great for window shopping'...'Ideal for the wheelchair user with its Shopmobility scheme'...have been just a few of the positive comments made by customers who compare the well-laid-out facility with the draughty, cold and wet shopping centre as it was before redevelopment. Most people in and around Uxbridge would agree that The Pavilions has fulfilled its original intention and its range of shops and services, its craft fairs, fashion shows and community activities, together with its inspiring and innovative design, has made the centre a focus for local life. Uxbridge, in fact, is not only becoming a mature regional centre but looks forward to a future in which the town is well able to compete with any in the surrounding area.

The reality of the completed Pavilions far exceeded people's expectations, and the magnificent shopping centre that eventually graced Uxbridge bore no resemblance to the original design that was typical of the stark style of building that was popular with the architects of the 1960s and 70s. Today's attractive and inviting complex has turned what used to be a chore into a pleasure! Many of the original tenants took the opportunity to refit their premises, and new lettings have extended the range of goods offered within the shopping centre. As part of the ongoing commitment to excellence of service, customers are asked to write in giving their views on the newly revamped centre. 'Wonderful'...'Eye catching design and polite and helpful staff'...'Well attended by

The Woodbridge Partnership - soliciting success in Uxbridge

Law has been practised in Uxbridge for over 200 years by one firm which now functions under the name, The WOODBRIDGE Partnership. The history of the firm can be traced back to its establishment in 1796 when King George III was on the throne and some 19 years before Napoleon was defeated at Waterloo!

After completing his training at the Inner Temple in London, John Hodder moved to Uxbridge and founded what was then a small family law firm. His office was at his 18th century home at 38 High Street. This Queen Anne property had an arched coach entrance which today has become the entrance to The Pavilions. The house remained the firm's office up until 1963 when they moved to Vine Street. In Uxbridge, Hodder found an up and coming country town with a developing infra-structure. By the time he had settled in, a bank had been opened in the town, a new market house was soon to be opened to cope with the increasing amount of trade, plans to provide paved

Above left: *Charles Woodbridge Junior (1851 - 1924).*
Above right: *A wage slip from 1938.*
Below: *The staff in 1938 in a picture taken at the rear of the premises.*

footways were underway, and already constructed was the Turnpike road from Brentford to Oxford. Uxbridge then, was the prime area to make a success of a new law firm and the survival of the firm for over 200 years is partly testimony to this.

One of John Hodder's Grandson's became a founding partner in the publishing firm, Hodder and Stoughton and his other Grandson, a civil servant, wrote the hymn, 'Thy word is like a garden, Lord'. These family accomplishments, impressive as they were, meant that when John Hodder left Uxbridge in 1809 without a suitable heir the law firm was passed on to a Norfolk man, Thomas H Riches. Ironically it was Riches, who took Charles Woodbridge Senior on as his partner in 1820, who therefore laid the foundation for the prominence of the Woodbridge family name throughout the firm's history.

By 1896, the year of the 100th anniversary of the firm, considerable progress had been made within the firm as well as within Uxbridge. The population of the town was now 3,154. The Magistrates Court now met in the Public Rooms once a week rather than only twice a month and a partner in the firm was now Clerk to the Justices. The County Court now met in the Public Rooms rather than at The George Inn as it had before and the two Registrars and High Bailiffs were both partners of the firm. Other partners of the firm held positions such as: Clerk to the Commissioners of Income Tax and Inhabited Home Duty; Superintendent Registrars of Births, Deaths and Marriages; Clerk to the Rural District Council; and Clerk and Treasurer of the Joint Hospital Board. A slightly more unusual appointment held by one of the partners at this time was, Commissioner for Taking the Acknowledgment of Deeds by Married Women! Algernon Rivers Woodbridge, a partner in the firm from 1894 to 1951 and the grandfather of the current partner, Anthony Woodbridge, played an active part in the local Uxbridge life and indeed, was even the Captain of Uxbridge Football Club in 1896!

1996 saw the Bicentenary of the Uxbridge firm of solicitors. This occasion was marked with a 200th Anniversary Party at Stoke Place County Club on Saturday 22nd of June. Anthony Woodbridge, a direct descendent of Charles Woodbridge, qualified in 1967 and is senior partner in the firm today. The firm is still based in Uxbridge and is now called, The WOODBRIDGE Partnership. Like his Grandfather, Anthony Woodbridge plays an active part in the community. He is the chairman of the Harrow and Hillingdon Health NHS Trust, the Honorary Solicitor to Age Concern in Hillingdon and one of the founder members of the Abbeyfield Uxbridge Society which provides support and accommodation for lonely, elderly people in Hillingdon. The WOODBRIDGE Partnership is a vibrant and growing business with net fees of over £1 million. The firm now has one office at 42 Windsor Street and employs 30 members of staff. The firm is looking forward to the next 100 years in Uxbridge and hopes to continue to uphold the same values of providing cost effective, efficient legal services to the local community as it has done for over 200 years.

Above: *A letter dating from 1935.*
Below: *The Partnership today. From left to right: Geraldine Horwood (partner), Shuba Mehta (Consultant), Nicholas Hampson (Partner), Anthony Woodbridge (Partner).*

The WOODBRIDGE Partnership

Tooled up for the next century

The 20th century was just six years old when the Hallewells - a dock worker and his formidable wife - had their second child, a boy Harold Stuart, who was to be the eldest boy in a family of seven brothers and one sister. Bright minded and inventive, Harold enjoyed working with his hands, and was eventually apprenticed as toolmaker to Listers in Dursley. Harold gained a wide experience in his chosen career with companies such as CAV, Ford, Weir Precision, Fairey Aviation and the Gramophone Company (today EMI). And with every step forward, the ambitious young man was creating a dream - to set up a toolmaking and engineering company, and be his own boss.

When war broke out in 1939, Harold and a number of his brothers continued to work in the reserved occupation of engineering. During the early 1940s he was able to buy a detached house in Hayes, and it was here that he began at last to realise his ambitions. He was eventually able to register his new company: Toolmasters Ltd. With his brother Raymond and other close colleagues, Harold rented premises at Hillingdon Heath, and immediately began to train a number of youngsters straight from school. The training of young people through apprenticeship to skilled toolmakers became - and still remains - company policy.

As the company expanded, larger premises were needed and Parkfield, an old stable building, was rented. Disaster struck Parkfield, however, when an unattended gas stove exploded during the night shift, causing extensive damage to the premises. This proved devastating to the young company, who were held liable for the damage. Toolmasters survived - just - though a further company, Mouldmasters Ltd, was registered just in case.... Mouldmasters produced moulds for the new plastic materials that were beginning to be developed.

Once war production was at an end, industry moved into new areas as people began to demand new consumer goods. At the time there were many small engineering works in competition with Toolmasters. Harold (known to most as HS) saw that in order to see progress it was vital to move into areas that were beyond the scope of rival companies. This meant acquiring machinery capable of machining larger components. A Victorian building, Connaught House, was bought, and a factory based on an old RAF hangar frame erected on the site of the old orchard. The house itself provided the company's offices.

Above: *Harold Hallewell, founder of the company.*
Below: *A 1950s works outing.*

The acquisition of Diaform, a product that accurately dressed profiles into grinding wheels, was a key move that brought about further expansion. Soon the company was exporting Diaform to the USA and other overseas markets.

During the 1950s the company became more structured, with HS as chairman and managing director, and steady growth followed the early formative years. A major design concept on the Diaform principle was patented in all the main industrial countries, simplifying the production of highly precise form ground components and removed possibilities of accidental operator errors. Space to house the expanding Diaform business was required, and in 1960 new premises were built in Uxbridge and the company was set fair for further achievement. In 1962 restructuring of the company saw Toolmasters Ltd as a holding company with two subsidiaries, Toolmasters (Manufacturing) Ltd and Diaform Ltd.

Sadly, Harold Hallewell died the following year, before seeing the full extent of his company's achievements, and Raymond became Group Chairman. A year after celebrating their Silver Jubilee in 1967, Diaform Ltd was granted the Queen's Award to Industry for Export Achievement. Toolmasters went from strength to strength during the 1970s, which saw the company move into the developing electronic age to provide the market with a numerically controlled Diaform machine.

The last decade of the 20th century proved difficult for the engineering manufacturing industry in the UK. Stiff competition from around the world led to a general down sizing in the industry, and in 1993 Toolmasters closed its premises on the Uxbridge Industrial Estate. Their commitment, however, remains the same - to squarely meet the challenge of the future. From starting life as a simple press tooling maker, Toolmasters begins the new millennium with a varied range of products that include a comprehensive range of machinery to the razor, industrial and medical blade industries, quality control equipment, precision grinding products and intricate tooling to various process industries.

Theirs, in fact, is the ongoing story of a successful family company which looks to build on its achievements in the years ahead with a sense of pride in the past and confidence in the future.

Above left: A CNC Diaform controlled high precision gear cutter grinding machine.
Top: The premises in the 1960s.
Below: The Uxbridge Road premises today.

The image of success

Photographers enjoy visiting Uxbridge. Every day large numbers of enthusiast and semi-professional photographers travel 10, 20, 25 miles or further to get there; but, fascinating though Uxbridge is, it is not the town itself which attracts them - it is the presence in High Road, Cowley, of the Euro Foto Centre, where they can browse at leisure through a huge range of stock ranging from the latest digital technology to traditional darkroom equipment.

Peter Randolph's idea of opening a large cash-and-carry photographic warehouse represented a radical new departure for the industry in 1968. Peter had been in the photography business for some years, having set up as a professional photographer shortly after his demob from the RAF. Trading as Pictorialist from the family home in Frays Avenue, West Drayton, Peter had set up a commercial photography studio. The business had grown and Peter and his wife Joan had taken premises in Horton Road, West Drayton, where they diversified into wholesale photofinishing; they then moved into retailing, and by the end of the decade there were Pictorialist shops in Uxbridge and Slough selling everything a keen amateur photographer was likely to need to develop and print his own photographs.

The abolition of the retail price maintenance in the late 1960s heralded greater competition in the retail trade. Peter quickly realised that the customers of the future were likely to shop around more before buying, and that price was going to be an important factor in deciding where they took their custom. He realised, too, that by setting up a self-service store he would be able to offer a comprehensive range of products, all at attractive discount prices; and so Pictorialist opened as a cash-and-carry in a three-storey house. At this time Peter's son, Paul, joined the business and started a mail order division as a convenient alternative for potential customers who lived further afield. Anything from a bottle of developer to a complete camera system could be delivered straight to the customer's door.

Left: *1950s - outside the Horton Road premises.*
Below: *The first company vehicle.*
Bottom: *Peter Randolph - 1948 Olympics photographer.*

The 1970s brought new technology, much of it from Japan, and there was a tremendous market for the new products. To cope with the escalating demand, Peter and Paul had a 10,000 square foot warehouse built, between Uxbridge and West Drayton which could be easily accessed from the motorway network. In 1975 the extensive new cash-and-carry warehouse opened as Euro Foto Centre, offering customers everything they could wish for: a huge range of goods all under one roof, at competitive prices, with expert and fully-trained staff on hand to provide advice on each product, and with refreshment facilities and ample car parking. This simple but winning formula has proved ideal as it can adapted easily to include each new market as it develops. The range of products today is wider than ever: specialist and niche market items have been joined by an impressive array of digital cameras and printers, camcorders, scanners, software and consumables. In-house training for the staff is complemented by supplier training, so that product managers are equally happy to demonstrate a product in the dedicated demonstration area, advise on the suitability of an item or process for a customer's own particular needs, or to answer technical queries about the specifications and capabilities of a specific brand. This ensures that whether customers are about to begin exploring the possibilities of digital imaging, or whether they are professionals looking for traditional high-quality darkroom equipment, they can be sure of finding the right product, at the right price, and as much technical advice as they need at Euro Foto Centre.

As many customers wish to upgrade their existing equipment, a trade-in service is also offered, and the store has an excellent reputation as a good source of reliable second-hand equipment. Many customers who return

time and time again find it advantageous to join the Euro Foto Club, which entitles them to a EFC Gold Card giving 10 per cent discount on purchases. Meanwhile the mail order service, which lapsed for a while, has now been given a new lease of life through the Internet; Euro Foto Centre has its own website (www.euro-foto.com), where customers can browse through some 300 pages of products and buy online.

The business is still owned and run by the Randolph family. Peter has retired but still retains the position of chairman. His son, Paul, (currently managing director) and his wife, Sarah, now run the business. In the past few years they have been joined by their son, George, who is IT director, with responsibilities which include designing and maintaining the company's website. George also designed and wrote the company's software package which includes a complete EPOS system and full backoffice facilities for ordering and administration. So the dynamic, forward-looking enterprise will continue the tradition which Peter began more than 50 years ago, using innovative marketing methods to bring the products of the future to the customers of the next millennium.

Above: *The opening of the new superstore in 1975.*
Right: *The extensive premises today.*

Three generations of success

Parsons Precision Ltd, one of the two founding companies of Parsons Bailey Stamp have put their continued success down to its reputation for " reliable delivery, fair prices and high quality". In these more modern times of the quick soundbite, the combined company, which was established when Parsons bought Bailey Stamp and Sons in 1998, condenses this into just three words - service and quality.

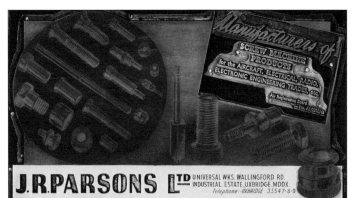

JR Parsons Ltd was founded in 1936 by Joe Parsons and his wife Lilian, in a bedroom at their home in Rayners Lane, Pinner. By this time Joe had amassed a deal of experience in the field of engineering, having started as a trainee gauge maker at the age of 16. Four years later he had spread his wings to a Swiss firm producing turned components. By 1936 the urge to go it alone became too much; Joe found the necessary £100 setting up costs and so began JR Parsons Ltd.

Perhaps flexibility played a large part in the success of the fledgling engineering works. The original business activity is cited as buying and selling "factoring". However with the onset of war, engineering became a crucial business and, through exceptionally busy twenty-four hour days, the firm concentrated entirely on equipment for aircraft makers, supporting the national war effort by making screws and parts for all the important aircraft of the day - The Spitfires, Wellingtons, Hawker Hunter and many others. By the sixties however, again willing to diversify with the times, the company branched out into an area few of us would automatically associate with precision engineering - manufacturing millions of studs for stiletto heels.

Diversification remains a strong point of the company, which lists among its main markets homewares, engineering tools, body jewellery and lighting. There seems no doubt that as new fields of engineering open up, Parsons Bailey Stamp will be there ready to fill the niche.

On the equipment and experience fronts, the combined company boasts the most up to date plant for producing high volume precision turned parts,

Above: *A printing plate of the 1950s.*
Below: *The inspection department in 1959.*

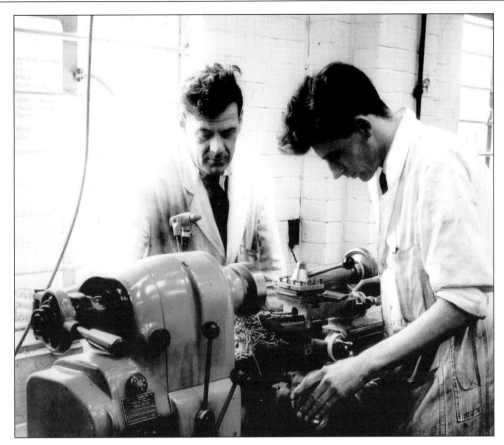

Silverdale Road, also in Hayes, before the final move to the Uxbridge Industrial Estate in 1950. These new premises were chosen as they offered opportunities for expansion. Indeed, since the move many extensions have been added, as the firm has developed.

Three generations of Parsons have, so far, been involved in the firm, and it is still regarded as a family business. However a high point for the company must have been the take-over of another long established and well-regarded family firm in the form of Bailey Stamp and Sons Ltd in 1998. The shareholders of Bailey Stamp wished to retire, and as both firms were leaders

plus over 110 years of producing subcontract turned parts. They count as a strength the fact that they are the longest established company of their type in Uxbridge, and worry not about competitors! They have held the British Standard EN ISO 9002 since 1988 for Quality Management Systems.

in the turned parts industry, it made sense to amalgamate at that point. Two separate companies - Parsons Precision and Bailey Stamp - retained the benefits of both their high-standard reputations by re-naming themselves as Parsons Bailey Stamp Ltd. The now joint operation continues to go from strength to strength, the bigger company being better placed to continue to succeed in a highly competitive field.

As this particular firm seems to have a finger in every possible engineering pie, just remember Parsons Bailey Stamp next time you decide to have your navel pierced or book your next trip by plane - you can be sure they had a hand in it somewhere!

Above left: An exhibition from the 1960s.
Top: The toolroom in the 1950s.
Below: A section of the main machine shop.

But it hasn't all been plain sailing for this now hugely successful company. An IOU from 1938 shows Joe Parsons borrowing £100 from Miss R Parsons at an interest rate of three and a half per cent per annum. Presumably Miss Parsons was well rewarded for her faith, but this was clearly not a risk-free investment; the Parsons were not born with the proverbial silver spoons in their mouths. Only Joe and Lilian's vision and hard work built the foundations of today's success.

Despite the very busy period during the forties, difficulties of a different kind hit them in the form of a fire which completely destroyed their war-time premises near the station in Hayes, in 1941. They quickly relocated to alternative premises in

The delights of flight

In the early years of the 20th century, aviation was a new phenomenon which seemed to many people utterly fantastic. However, Denham's first introduction to aeroplanes took place in an all too real context, with the arrival of the Royal Flying Corps No 5 and No 6 School of Aeronautics in the first world war. Airmen were taught how to rig aircraft, which meant aligning the wings and wiring them in position, and also how to pack parachutes in sheds on a site which later became the Martin Baker aircraft factory in Higher Denham. Various biplanes, of types that were used in France in the war, flew from the present aerodrome site, and the adjoining farm was used as a billet for the Commanding Officer.

After the war the land returned to farming, although it is known that Edward, Prince of Wales (later Edward VIII) flew to Denham in a twin engined de Havilland biplane to play golf. About this time Mr J M Bickerton, an ophthalmic surgeon who had been a Surgeon Lieutenant in the Royal Navy in the First World War, bought the field in Denham and started to fly from it. The grass was kept short in the early days by a flock of Jacob's Spanish sheep, and a shepherd and his dog rounded them up each morning to make way for the aeroplanes. The airfield attracted coverage in the national press when a garden party was held there in 1935 to celebrate the Silver Jubilee of George V and Queen Mary. Many guests flew in, including one who came in an autogyro. There were flying displays and a fleet of aircraft gave joy rides.

Some hangars were built to shelter Mr Bickerton's plane and others belonging to businessmen and enthusiasts, these aeroplanes were all chiefly made of wood and linen and needed protection from the weather. His first aeroplane was a de Havilland Moth, G-ABAG, which is now in the Shuttleworth Collection, and his second a Miles Hawk Major, G-ACYO. In 1938 the Aerodrome became a limited company and it was granted a licence.

The threat of another war increased military interest in aviation. The London University Air Squadron, the Volunteer Reserve Flying School from Heston, the Civil Air Guard School of Flying, and the Gladiator Aerobatic Team from Hendon became regular visitors to the airfield. After the fall of Dunkirk the aerodrome was requisitioned by the RAF who made many alterations, including the construction of nissen huts and blister hangars, and expansion of the site onto the neighbouring golf course and across the road. WAAF and RAF personnel were billeted nearby while the sheep were evacuated to a farm

Above left: *Mr Bickerton.*
Below: *A training aeroplane over Buckinghamshire.*

near High Wycombe. A flying training school moved in, which used de Havilland Tiger Moths and Miles Magisters, and was responsible for training many of the Arnhem glider pilots.

The post war years saw the airfield abandoned by the RAF to the mercy of vandals and looters. Ideas were put forward to turn the site into a gravel pit, a refuse dump, a housing estate, a mental hospital or even a prison. However, the Company restored the Aerodrome and eventually civil flying recommenced.

Since that time a great many flying organisations and aviation companies have made Denham their base at different periods. These have included Denham Aero Club, Airways Aero Club, The Spartan Flyers, CSE, Air Gregory, the Air Training Corps Squadron 2370, The Lapwing Flying Group, the BBC flying club, HeliAir, The Lynton Group and The Pilot Centre. At the time of writing Cabair

has had the Denham School of Flying for some 20 years and is known for helping their flying instructors to become airline pilots as well as teaching people to fly.

Well-known figures associated with the Aerodrome over the years include Air Vice Marshall Sir Ivor Broome who was forced by the weather to land in a Blenheim and later became President of the ATC Squadron; Douglas Bader, who visited while a film was being made of his remarkable life; former British free-style Aerobatic Champion Brian Lecomber, who learned to fly there; the owner of Air Gregory who was once Stirling Moss' manager; Quentin Smith who flew round the world in a very small helicopter in 1997; and many other celebrities, some associated with the nearby Denham film studios. As for the aircraft themselves, almost every small type must have passed through the Aerodrome at some time.

The second half of the 20th century saw many improvements, including the installation of electric landing lights and the tarmacing of the runway, and the establishment of a small restaurant now called 'Biggles'. With the easing of border controls in the 1980s, small aircraft can travel without notice to countries within the EC and foreign visitors may more readily visit Denham. Plans for the future of the Aerodrome include the provision of better visitor and spectator facilities so that more people can share in the excitement of watching the aircraft - or even take a trial flying lesson to see what flying over the countryside is like for themselves!

Above: *A business helicopter.*
Top: *Denham Aerodrome.*

A sunny September day in 1936 has attracted children, like bees to a honeypot, to the paddling pool in Uxbridge Recreation Ground,

A scene from the Uxbridge
Show in 1935.

Acknowledgments

Hillingdon Heritage Service

Irene Lovelock

Caroline Cotton

David Varley

Tanya Britton

Thanks are also due to Peggy Burns for penning the editorial text and

Margaret Wakefield for her copywriting skills.